Literary Laurels

KIDS' EDITION

*A Reader's Guide to
Award-Winning Children's Books*

EDITED BY

Laura Carlson
Sean Creighton
Sheila Cunningham

HILLYARD
New York

Literary Laurels
Hillyard Industries, Inc.
302 West 12th Street
New York, NY, 10014
(212) 255-3553

Printed and bound in the United States of America

9 8 7 6 5 4 3 2 1

ISBN 0-9647361-1-X

Literary Laurels

KIDS' EDITION

Introduction

٢٩

Here is a handy and practical guide to help you easily choose a book for a child. As a parent, grandparent, or family friend, you need help navigating the vast, confusing world of children's books. Which story is appropriate for a 10-year-old? Should it be silly or serious? Fact or fiction? Which authors write books with timeless themes? Which books are really popular with children across the country?

Literary Laurels: Kids' Edition presents carefully chosen lists of more than 1,200 award-winning children's books. The roster was culled from hundreds of book-prize competitions covering thousands of titles. *Literary Laurels'* aim is to provide a clear, easy-to-use catalog of titles which are most popular with the librarians, educators, writers, and even children who vote for the best books each year. But particular care has been taken to provide diversity of subject matter, to appeal to different age groups, and to include foreign, British, and Canadian favorites as well.

Here you will find such well-known prizes as the Caldecott and Newbery medals (including their honor books), as well as the Laura Ingalls Wilder and Hans Christian Andersen awards. You will also discover many other delightful lists saluting:

- social values (Jane Addams Award, Coretta Scott King Award)
- international books (Smarties Prize, Mildred L. Batchelder Award)
- genres (Western Heritage Award, Scott O'Dell Award for Historical Fiction)
- history and science (*Orbis Pictus* Prize, New York Academy of Sciences Award)

The lists are complete from the inception of each award, where practical, and one even includes books published as far back as 1863 with *The Water Babies*. Each list is enhanced with brief text which explains the gist and history of the award. Furthermore, *Literary Laurels: Kids' Edition* provides useful indexes as well as a roster of books which have won numerous kudos.

How do you match the right book to the child? Try these suggestions:

- locate a fitting category on the contents page, then peruse the lists featured
- search the indexes for a favorite author or title, then choose another from its award list
- consult "Above the Rest"—a list of multiple-award winners—for ideas
- browse a list or two and recall old favorites

Like its grown-up counterpart, *Literary Laurels: A Reader's Guide to Award-Winning Fiction,* let this new *Kids' Edition* be your handbook for a book to recommend, to buy, to add to a library, or to read yourself.

Contents

ૐ

Contents

Awards by Category and Age

۶&

Most winning children's books are fiction. But many award lists also include biographies, histories, and other types of writing. Here are lists arranged by category. Where possible, awards have also been grouped by age appeal.

SPECIALITY AREAS

Biography

Body of Work

Children's Choice

Classics

History

International

Mystery

Picture Books

Poetry

Romance

Science

Social Values

Western

AGE APPEAL
Very Young

Ages 4 to 8

Ages 9 to 13

Ages 13 to 18

ABBY Award

ॐ

This award, whose name is an acronym for the American Booksellers Book of the Year, results from surveying thousands of booksellers for the book "they most love to recommend." Winners receive $5,000 when the award is presented at the American Booksellers Association annual convention. The award was launched in 1991, and the stories often have a moral.

1995   *The Rainbow Fish,* Marcus Pfister

1994   *Stellaluna,* Janell Cannon

1993   *Old Turtle,* Douglas Wood

1992   *Brother Eagle, Sister Sky: A Message from Chief Seattle,* Susan Jeffers

1991   *The Education of Little Tree,* Forrest Carter

Jane Addams Children's Book Award

☙

Peace, social justice, and world community are themes featured in the winners of this award. Its namesake, Jane Addams, was a social reformer who shared the 1931 Nobel Peace Prize for her work with underprivileged and oppressed woman and children, particularly immigrants. She founded Hull-House in Chicago, America's best-known settlement house. The prize is given each September by the Women's International League for Peace and Freedom and the Jane Addams Peace Association.

1995   *Kids at Work: Lewis Hine and the Crusade Against Child Labor,* Russell Freedman

1994   *Freedom's Children: Young Civil Rights Activists Tell Their Own Stories,* Ellen Levine

1993   *A Taste of Salt: A Story of Modern Haiti,* Frances Temple

1992   *Journey of the Sparrows,* Fran Leeper Buss, assisted by Daisy Cubias

1991   *The Big Book for Peace,* ed. by Ann Durell and Marilyn Sachs

1990   *A Long Hard Journey: The Story of the Pullman Porter,* Patricia C. McKissack and Fredrick McKissack

1989   *Looking Out,* Victoria Boutis

1988   *Waiting for the Rain: A Novel of South Africa,* Sheila Gordon

1987   *Nobody Wants a Nuclear War,* Judith Vigna

1986   *Ain't Gonna Study War No More: The Story of America's Peace Seekers,* Milton Meltzer

1985   *The Short Life of Sophie Scholl,* Hermann Vinke, trans. from German by Hedwig Patcher

1984 *Rain of Fire*, Marion Dane Bauer

1983 *Hiroshima No Pika*, Toshi Maruki

1982 *A Spirit to Ride the Whirlwind*, Athena V. Lord

1981 *First Woman in Congress: Jeannette Rankin*, Florence White

1980 *The Road from Home: The Story of an Armenian Girl*, David Kherdian

1979 *Many Smokes, Many Moons*, Jamake Highwater

1978 *Child of the Owl*, Laurence Yep

1977 *Never to Forget: The Jews of the Holocaust*, Milton Meltzer

1976 *Paul Robeson*, Eloise Greenfield

1975 *The Princess and the Admiral*, Charlotte Pomerantz

1974 *Nilda*, Nicholasa Mohr

1973 *The Riddle of Racism*, S. Carl Hirsch

1972 *The Tamarack Tree*, Betty Underwood

1971 *Jane Addams: Pioneer of Social Justice*, Cornelia L. Meigs

1970 No award

1969 *The Endless Steppe: Growing Up in Siberia*, Esther Hautzig

1968 *The Little Fishes*, Erik Christian Haugaard

1967 *Queenie Peavy*, Robert Burch

1966 *Berries Goodman*, Emily Cheney Neville

1965 *Meeting with a Stranger*, Duane Bradley

1964 *Profiles in Courage*, John F. Kennedy

1963 *The Monkey and the Wild, Wild Wind*, Ryerson Johnson

1962 *The Road to Agra*, Aimee Sommerfelt

1961 *"What then, Raman?"*, Shirley L. Aurora

1960 *Champions of Peace,* Edith Patterson Meyer

1959 No award

1958 *The Perilous Road,* William O. Steele

1957 *Blue Mystery,* Margot Benary-Isbert

1956 *Story of the Negro,* Arna Bontemps

1955 *Rainbow Round the World,* Elizabeth Yates

1954 *Stick-in-the-Mud,* Jean Ketchum

1953 *People Are Important,* Eva Knox Evans

Hans Christian Andersen Award

ও

Popularly known as the "Little Nobel," this international prize is the most distinguished in children's literature. It is named for the nineteenth-century Danish author of such memorable and inspirational fairy tales as "The Ugly Duckling" and "The Red Shoes." This award honors the entire work of authors and illustrators, not individual titles, and is granted by an international jury selected by IBBY (International Board on Books for Young People). Since 1956, a gold medal and diploma have been awarded every other year.

Author

1996   Uri Orlev (Israel)

1994   Michio Mado (Japan)

1992   Virginia Hamilton (USA)

1990   Tormod Haugen (Norway)

1988   Annie M.G. Schmidt (Netherlands)

1986   Patricia Wrightson (Australia)

1984   Christine Nöstlinger (Austria)

1982   Lygia Bojunga Nunes (Brazil)

1980   Bohumil Ríha (Czechoslovakia)

1978   Paula Fox (USA)

1976   Cecil Bodker (Denmark)

1974   Maria Gripe (Sweden)

1972   Scott O'Dell (USA)

1970   Gianni Rodari (Italy)

1968   James Krüss (Germany)
       José Maria Sanchez-Silva (Spain)

1966   Tove Jansson (Finland)

1964   René Guillot (France)

1962   Meindert DeJong (USA)

1960   Erich Kästner (Germany)

1958   Astrid Lindgren (Sweden)

1956   Eleanor Farjeon (Great Britain)

Illustrator

1996   Klaus Ensikat (Germany)

1994   Jörg Müller (Switzerland)

1992   Kveta Pacovská (Czechoslovakia)

1990   Lisbeth Zwerger (Austria)

1988   Dusan Kallay (Czechoslovakia)

1986   Robert Ingpen (Australia)

1984   Mitsumasa Anno (Japan)

1982   Zbigniew Rychlicki (Poland)

1980   Suekichi Akaba (Japan)

1978   Svend Otto S. (Denmark)

1976   Tatjana Mawrina (USSR)

1974   Farshid Mesghali (Iran)

1972   Ib Spang Ohlsson (Denmark)

1970   Maurice Sendak (USA)

1968   Jiri Trnka (Czechoslovakia)

1966   Alois Carigiet (Switzerland)

Mildred L. Batchelder Award

ॐ

An outstanding foreign-language book, subsequently published in English, is cited by this award, which has been given annually since 1968. The award aims to promote the international exchange of quality children's books. It is sponsored by the American Library Association, which honors in its name a beloved past executive director of its children's services division. Winning titles appeal to children from preschool to teens.

1996 *The Lady with the Hat,* Uri Orlev, trans. from Hebrew by Hillel Halkin

1995 *The Boys from St. Petri,* Bjarne Reuter, trans. from Danish by Anthea Bell

1994 *The Apprentice,* Pilar Molina Llorente, trans. from Spanish by Robin Longshaw

1993 No award

1992 *The Man from the Other Side,* Uri Orlev, trans. from Hebrew by Hillel Halkin

1991 *A Hand Full of Stars,* Rafik Schami, trans. from German by Rika Lesser

1990 *Buster's World,* Bjarne Reuter, trans. from Danish by Anthea Bell

1989 *Crutches,* Peter Härtling, trans. from German by Elizabeth D. Crawford

1988 *If You Didn't Have Me,* Ulf Nilsson, trans. from Swedish by George Blecher and Lone Thygesen-Blecher

1987 *No Hero for the Kaiser,* Rudolph Frank, trans. from German by Patricia Crampton

1986 *Rose Blanche,* Christopher Gallaz and Roberto Innocenti, trans. from French by Martha Coventry and Richard Graglia

1985 *The Island on Bird Street,* Uri Orlev, trans. from Hebrew by Hillel Halkin

1984 *Ronia, the Robber's Daughter,* Astrid Lindgren, trans. from Swedish by Patricia Crampton

1983 *Hiroshima No Pika,* Toshi Maruki, trans. from Japanese through the Kurita-Bando Literary Agency

1982 *The Battle Horse,* Harry Kullman, trans. from Swedish by George Blecher and Lone Thygesen-Blecher

1981 *The Winter When Time Was Frozen,* Els Pelgrom, trans. from Dutch by Maryka Rudnik and Raphael Rudnik

1980 *The Sound of the Dragon's Feet,* Aliki Zei, trans. from Greek by Edward Fenton

1979 *Konrad,* Christine Nöstlinger, trans. from German by Anthea Bell
      Rabbit Island, Jörg Steiner, trans. from German by Ann Conrad Lammers

1978 No award

1977 *The Leopard,* Cecil Bodker, trans. from Danish by Gunnar Poulsen

1976 *The Cat and Mouse Who Shared a House,* Ruth Hürlimann, trans. from German by Anthea Bell

1975 *An Old Tale Carved out of Stone,* A. Linevski, trans. from Russian by Maria Polushkin

1974 *Petros' War,* Aliki Zei, trans. from Greek by Edward Fenton

1973 *Pulga,* S.R. Van Iterson, trans. from Dutch by Alexander Gode and Alison Gode

1972 *Friedrich,* Hans Peter Richter, trans. from German by Edite Kroll

1971 *In the Land of Ur: The Discovery of Ancient Mesopotamia,* Hans Baumann, trans. from German by Stella Humphries

1970 *Wildcat under Glass,* Aliki Zei, trans. from Greek by Edward Fenton

1969 *Don't Take Teddy,* Babbis Friis-Baastad, trans. from Norwegian by Lise Somme McKinnon

1968 *The Little Man,* Erich Kästner, trans. from German by James Kirkup

Boston Globe–Horn Book Award

ે

Librarians in New England judge these the best fiction, nonfiction, and illustrated books of the year. Sponsored by *The Boston Globe*, Boston's major newspaper, and *The Horn Book*, a well-known children's magazine, this award is given in the autumn and consists of a silver bowl and $500.

Fiction

1995   *Some of the Kinder Planets*, Tim Wynne-Jones

1994   *Scooter*, Vera B. Williams

1993   *Ajeemah and His Son*, James Berry

1992   *Missing May*, Cynthia Rylant

1991   *The True Confessions of Charlotte Doyle*, Avi, illus. Ruth E. Murray

1990   *Maniac Magee*, Jerry Spinelli

1989   *The Village by the Sea*, Paula Fox

1988   *The Friendship*, Mildred D. Taylor, illus. Max Ginsburg

1987   *Rabble Starkey*, Lois Lowry

1986   *In Summer Light*, Zibby Oneal

1985   *The Moves Make the Man*, Bruce Brooks

1984   *A Little Fear*, Patricia Wrightson

1983   *Sweet Whispers, Brother Rush*, Virginia Hamilton

1982   *Playing Beatie Bow*, Ruth Park

1981   *The Leaving*, Lynn Hall

1980   *Conrad's War*, Andrew Davies

1979   *Humbug Mountain*, Sid Fleischman

1978   *The Westing Game*, Ellen Raskin

1977   *Child of the Owl*, Laurence Yep

1976   *Unleaving*, Jill Paton Walsh

1975   *Transport 7-41-R*, T. Degens

1974   *M.C. Higgins, the Great*, Virginia Hamilton

1973   *The Dark Is Rising*, Susan Cooper

1972   *Tristan and Iseult*, Rosemary Sutcliff

1971   *A Room Made of Windows*, Eleanor Cameron

1970   *The Intruder*, John Rowe Townsend

1969   *A Wizard of Earthsea*, Ursula K. Le Guin

1968   *The Spring Rider*, John Lawson

1967   *The Little Fishes*, Erik Christian Haugaard

Nonfiction

1995   *Abigail Adams: Witness to a Revolution*, Natalie S. Bober

1994   *Eleanor Roosevelt: A Life of Discovery*, Russell Freedman

1993   *Sojourner Truth: Ain't I a Woman?*, Patricia C. McKissack and Fredrick McKissack

1992   *Talking with Artists*, Pat Cummings

1991   *Appalachia: The Voices of Sleeping Birds*, Cynthia Rylant, illus. Barry Moser

1990   *The Great Little Madison*, Jean Fritz

1989   *The Way Things Work*, David Macaulay

1988   *Anthony Burns: The Defeat and Triumph of a Fugitive Slave,*
        Virginia Hamilton

1987   *The Pilgrims of Plimouth,*   Marcia Sewall

1986   *Auks, Rocks, and the Odd Dinosaur: Inside Stories from the
        Smithsonian's Museum of Natural History,*   Peggy Thomson

1985   *Commodore Perry in the Land of the Shogun,*   Rhoda
        Blumberg

1984   *The Double Life of Pocahontas,*   Jean Fritz, illus. Ed Young

1983   *Behind Barbed Wire: The Imprisonment of Japanese Americans
        During World War II,*   Daniel S. Davis

1982   *Upon the Head of a Goat: A Childhood in Hungary 1939–1944,*
        Aranka Siegal

1981   *The Weaver's Gift,*   Kathryn Lasky, illus. Christopher G.
        Knight

1980   *Building: The Fight Against Gravity,*   Mario Salvadori, illus.
        Saralinda Hooker and Christopher Ragus

1979   *The Road from Home: The Story of an Armenian Girl,*   David
        Kherdian

1978   *Mischling, Second Degree: My Childhood in Nazi Germany,*
        Ilse Koehn

1977   *Chance, Luck and Destiny,*   Peter Dickinson, illus. Victor G.
        Ambrus and David Smee

1976   *Voyaging to Cathay: Americans in the China Trade,*   Shirley
        Glubok and Alfred Tamarin

Picture Book

1995   *John Henry,*   Julius Lester, illus. Jerry Pinkney

1994   *Grandfather's Journey,*   Allen Say

1993 *The Fortune-Tellers,* Lloyd Alexander, illus. Trina Schart Hyman

1992 *Seven Blind Mice,* Ed Young

1991 *The Tale of the Mandarin Ducks,* Katherine Paterson, illus. Leo Dillon and Diane Dillon

1990 *Lon Po Po: A Red-Riding Hood Story from China,* Ed Young

1989 *Shy Charles,* Rosemary Wells

1988 *The Boy of the Three-Year Nap,* Dianne Snyder, illus. Allen Say

1987 *Mufaro's Beautiful Daughters: An African Tale,* John Steptoe

1986 *The Paper Crane,* Molly Bang

1985 *Mama Don't Allow,* Thacher Hurd

1984 *Jonah and the Great Fish,* Warwick Hutton

1983 *A Chair for My Mother,* Vera B. Williams

1982 *A Visit to William Blake's Inn: Poems for Innocent and Experienced Travelers,* Nancy Willard, illus. Alice Provensen and Martin Provensen

1981 *Outside Over There,* Maurice Sendak

1980 *The Garden of Abdul Gasazi,* Chris Van Allsburg

1979 *The Snowman,* Raymond Briggs

1978 *Anno's Journey,* Mitsumasa Anno

1977 *Granfa' Grig Had a Pig and Other Rhymes Without Reason from Mother Goose,* Wallace Tripp

1976 *Thirteen,* Jerry Joyner and Remy Charlip

1975 *Anno's Alphabet: An Adventure in Imagination,* Mitsumasa Anno

1974 *Jambo Means Hello: Swahili Alphabet Book,* Muriel Feelings, illus. Tom Feelings

1973 *King Stork,* Howard Pyle, illus. Trina Schart Hyman

1972 *Mr. Gumpy's Outing,* John Burningham

1971 *If I Built a Village,* Kazue Mizumura

1970 *Hi, Cat!,* Ezra Jack Keats

1969 *The Adventures of Paddy Pork,* John S. Goodall

1968 *Tikki Tikki Tembo,* Arlene Mosel, illus. Blair Lent

1967 *London Bridge Is Falling Down!,* Peter Spier

Caldecott Medal

❧

Distinguished American children's picture books are celebrated by this award, which is administered by the American Library Association. It is named for the nineteenth-century English illustrator Randolph Caldecott, who authored and illustrated *The House That Jack Built* among other well-loved books. Awarded in February, the award is considered one of the highest achievements in children's literature.

1996 *Officer Buckle and Gloria,* Peggy Rathmann

1995 *Smoky Night,* Eve Bunting, illus. David Diaz

1994 *Grandfather's Journey,* Allen Say

1993 *Mirette on the High Wire,* Emily Arnold McCully

1992 *Tuesday,* David Wiesner

1991 *Black and White,* David Macaulay

1990 *Lon Po Po: A Red-Riding Hood Story from China,* Ed Young

1989 *Song and Dance Man,* Karen Ackerman, illus. Stephen Gammell

1988 *Owl Moon,* Jane Yolen, illus. John Schoenherr

1987 *Hey, Al!,* Arthur Yorinks, illus. Richard Egielski

1986 *The Polar Express,* Chris Van Allsburg

1985 *Saint George and the Dragon,* retold by Margaret Hodges, illus. Trina Schart Hyman

1984 *The Glorious Flight: Across the Channel with Louis Blériot,* Alice Provensen and Martin Provensen

1983 *Shadow,* Blaise Cendrars, trans. and illus. Marcia Brown

1982 *Jumanji,* Chris Van Allsburg

1981 *Fables,* Arnold Lobel

1980 *Ox-Cart Man,* Donald Hall, illus. Barbara Cooney

1979 *The Girl Who Loved Wild Horses,* Paul Goble

1978 *Noah's Ark,* Peter Spier

1977 *Ashanti to Zulu,* Margaret Musgrove, illus. Leo Dillon and Diane Dillon

1976 *Why Mosquitoes Buzz in People's Ears,* retold by Verna Aardema, illus. Leo Dillon and Diane Dillon

1975 *Arrow to the Sun,* Gerald McDermott

1974 *Duffy and the Devil,* retold by Harve Zemach, illus. Margot Zemach

1973 *The Funny Little Woman,* retold by Arlene Mosel, illus. Blair Lent

1972 *One Fine Day,* Nonny Hogrogian

1971 *A Story, a Story,* Gail E. Haley

1970 *Sylvester and the Magic Pebble,* William Steig

1969 *The Fool of the World and the Flying Ship,* retold by Arthur Ransome, illus. Uri Shulevitz

1968 *Drummer Hoff,* adapted by Barbara Emberley, illus. Ed Emberley

1967 *Sam, Bangs & Moonshine,* Evaline Ness

1966 *Always Room for One More,* Sorche Nic Leodhas, illus. Nonny Hogrogian

1965 *May I Bring a Friend?,* Beatrice Schenk de Regniers, illus. Beni Montresor

1964 *Where the Wild Things Are*, Maurice Sendak

1963 *The Snowy Day*, Ezra Jack Keats

1962 *Once a Mouse*, Marcia Brown

1961 *Baboushka and the Three Kings*, Ruth Robbins, illus. Nicolas Sidjakov

1960 *Nine Days to Christmas*, Marie Hall Ets and Aurora Labastida

1959 *Chanticleer and the Fox*, Barbara Cooney

1958 *Time of Wonder*, Robert McCloskey

1957 *A Tree Is Nice*, Janice Udry, illus. Marc Simont

1956 *Frog Went A-Courtin'*, retold by John Langstaff, illus. Feodor Rojankovsky

1955 *Cinderella*, retold by and illus. Marcia Brown

1954 *Madeline's Rescue*, Ludwig Bemelmans

1953 *The Biggest Bear*, Lynd Ward

1952 *Finders Keepers*, Will Lipkind, illus. Nicolas Mordvinoff

1951 *The Egg Tree*, Katherine Milhous

1950 *Song of the Swallows*, Leo Politi

1949 *The Big Snow*, Berta Hader and Elmer Hader

1948 *White Snow, Bright Snow*, Alvin Tresselt, illus. Roger Duvoisin

1947 *The Little Island*, Golden MacDonald, illus. Leonard Weisgard

1946 *The Rooster Crows*, Maude Petersham and Miska Petersham

1945 *Prayer for a Child*, Rachel Field, illus. Elizabeth Orton Jones

1944 *Many Moons*, James Thurber, illus. Louis Slobodkin

1943 *The Little House*, Virginia Lee Burton

1942   *Make Way for Ducklings,* Robert McCloskey

1941   *They Were Strong and Good,* Robert Lawson

1940   *Abraham Lincoln,* Ingri d'Aulaire and Edgar Parin d'Aulaire

1939   *Mei Li,* Thomas Handforth

1938   *Animals of the Bible,* Helen Dean Fish, illus. Dorothy P. Lathrop

Caldecott Honor Books

ஃ

Runners-up for the distinction of being the best American picture book of the year are often as popular with children and adults as are the medal winners. Their book jackets proudly bear a foil sticker that sets them apart from other picture books. Because of their large number, just ten years' worth of books are included here.

1996 *Alphabet City,* Stephen T. Johnson
      Zin! Zin! Zin! a Violin, Lloyd Moss, illus. Marjorie Priceman
      The Faithful Friend, Robert D. San Souci, illus. Brian Pinkney
      Tops & Bottoms, Janet Stevens

1995 *John Henry,* Julius Lester, illus. Jerry Pinkney
      Swamp Angel, Anne Isaacs, illus. Paul O. Zelinsky
      Time Flies, Eric Rohmann

1994 *In the Small, Small Pond,* Denise Fleming
      Owen, Kevin Henkes
      Peppe the Lamplighter, Elisa Bartone, illus. Ted Lewin
      Raven: A Trickster Tale from the Pacific Northwest, Gerald McDermott
      Yo! Yes? Christopher Raschka

1993 *Seven Blind Mice,* Ed Young
      The Stinky Cheese Man and Other Fairly Stupid Tales, Jon Scieszka, illus. Lane Smith
      Working Cotton, Sherley Anne Williams, illus. Carole Byard

1992 *Tar Beach,* Faith Ringgold

1991 *"More, More, More," Said the Baby: 3 Love Stories,* Vera B. Williams
      Puss in Boots, Charles Perrault, trans. Malcom Arthur, illus. Fred Marcellino

1990   *Bill Peet: An Autobiography,* Bill Peet
          Color Zoo, Lois Ehlert
          Hershel and the Hanukkah Goblins, Eric Kimmel, illus. Trina Schart Hyman
          The Talking Eggs, Robert D. San Souci, illus. Jerry Pinkney

1989   *The Boy of the Three-Year Nap,* Dianne Snyder, illus. Allen Say
          Free Fall, David Wiesner
          Goldilocks and the Three Bears, James Marshall
          Mirandy and Brother Wind, Patricia C. McKissack, illus. Jerry Pinkney

1988   *Mufaro's Beautiful Daughters: An African Tale,* John Steptoe

1987   *Alphabatics,* Suse MacDonald
          Rumpelstiltskin, Paul O. Zelinsky
          The Village of Round and Square Houses, Ann Grifalconi

Carnegie Medal

ࢠ

Fiction published first in the United Kingdom is here honored by the British Library Association. Aggressive publicity soon makes winning books popular elsewhere in the English-speaking world. The medal was first granted in 1936 to honor the hundredth birthday of Andrew Carnegie, the impoverished Scot who emigrated to America and made a fortune in steel. His subsequent philanthropies focused on public libraries and education in both America and the U.K.

1994   *Whispers in the Graveyard,* Theresa Breslin

1993   *Stone Cold,* Robert Swindells

1992   *Flour Babies,* Anne Fine

1991   *Dear Nobody,* Berlie Doherty

1990   *Wolf,* Gillian Cross

1989   *Goggle-eyes,* Anne Fine

1988   *A Pack of Lies,* Geraldine McCaughrean

1987   *The Ghost Drum,* Susan Price

1986   *Granny Was a Buffer Girl,* Berlie Doherty

1985   *Storm,* Kevin Crossley-Holland, illus. Alan Marks

1984   *The Changeover,* Margaret Mahy

1983   *Handles,* Jan Mark, illus. David Parkins

1982   *The Haunting,* Margaret Mahy

1981   *The Scarecrows,* Robert Westall

1980   *City of Gold and Other Stories from the Old Testament,* Peter Dickinson, illus. Michael Foreman

1979 *Tulku,* Peter Dickinson

1978 *The Exeter Blitz,* David Rees

1977 *The Turbulent Term of Tyke Tiler,* Gene Kemp, illus. Carolyn Dinan

1976 *Thunder and Lightnings,* Jan Mark, illus. Jim Russell

1975 *The Machine Gunners,* Robert Westall

1974 *The Stronghold,* Mollie Hunter

1973 *The Ghost of Thomas Kempe,* Penelope Lively, illus. Antony Maitland

1972 *Watership Down,* Richard Adams

1971 *Josh,* Ivan Southall

1970 *The God Beneath the Sea,* Leon Garfield and Edward Blishen, illus. Charles Keeping

1969 *The Edge of the Cloud,* Kathleen Peyton, illus. Victor G. Ambrus

1968 *The Moon in the Cloud,* Rosemary Harris

1967 *The Owl Service,* Alan Garner

1966 No award

1965 *The Grange at High Force,* Philip Turner, illus. William Papas

1964 *Nordy Bank,* Sheena Porter, illus. Annette Macarthur-Onslow

1963 *Time of Trial,* Hester Burton, illus. Victor G. Ambrus

1962 *The Twelve and the Genii,* Pauline Clarke, illus. Cecil Leslie

1961 *A Stranger at Green Knowe,* Lucy M. Boston, illus. Peter Boston

1960 *The Making of Man,* Ian Wolfram Cornwall, illus M. Maitland Howard

1959 *The Lantern Bearers,* Rosemary Sutcliff, illus. Charles Keeping

1958   *Tom's Midnight Garden,* A. Philippa Pearce, illus. Susan Einzig

1957   *A Grass Rope,* William Mayne, illus. Lynton Lamb

1956   *The Last Battle,* C.S. Lewis, illus. Pauline Baynes

1955   *The Little Bookroom: Eleanor Farjeon's Short Stories for Children Chosen by Herself,* Eleanor Farjeon, illus. Edward Ardizzone

1954   *Knight Crusader,* Ronald Welch, illus. William Stobbs

1953   *A Valley Grows Up,* Edward Osmond

1952   *The Borrowers,* Mary Norton, illus. Diana Stanley

1951   *The Wool-Pack,* Cynthia Harnett

1950   *The Lark on the Wing,* Elfrida Vipont Foulds, illus. Terence Reginald Freeman

1949   *The Story of Your Home,* Agnes Allen, illus. Agnes Allen and Jack Allen

1948   *Sea Change,* Richard Armstrong, illus. Michael Leszczynski

1947   *Collected Stories for Children,* Walter de la Mare, illus. Irene Hawkins

1946   *The Little White Horse,* Elizabeth Goudge, illus. C. Walter Hodges

1945   No award

1944   *The Wind on the Moon,* Eric Linklater, illus. Nicolas Bentley

1943   No award

1942   *The Little Grey Men: A Story for the Young in Heart,* Denys James Watkins-Pitchford

1941   *We Couldn't Leave Dinah,* Mary Treadgold, illus. Stuart Tresilian

1940 *Visitors from London,* Kitty Barne, illus. Ruth Gervis

1939 *The Radium Woman: A Youth Edition of the Life of Madame Curie,* Eleanor Doorly, illus. Robert Gibbings

1938 *The Circus Is Coming,* Noel Streatfield, illus. Steven Spurrier

1937 *The Family from One End Street and Some of Their Adventures,* Eve Garnett

1936 *Pigeon Post,* Arthur Ransome

Lewis Carroll Shelf Award

ॐ

Well-loved children's classics are highlighted by this book award. First bestowed in 1958, this honor cited titles that were deemed of "sufficient quality to sit on the same bookshelf with *Alice in Wonderland,*" written by the award's namesake. The unanimous vote of a team of editors, librarians, teachers, parents, and writers was required to win this honor, which was, unfortunately, suspended in 1979 due to the award-founder's illness. However, books on this list still promise to fulfill the judges' requirement that they will appeal "to children 50 or even 100 years from now."

1979   *The Chocolate War,*   Robert Cormier, illus. Robert Vickery
        Dragonwings,   Laurence Yep
        The Island of the Grass King: The Further Adventures of Anatole,   Nancy Willard, illus. David McPhail
        Lyle, Lyle, Crocodile,   Bernard Waber
        The Road from Home: The Story of an Armenian Girl,   David Kherdian
        The Snowman,   Raymond Briggs
        A Wizard of Earthsea,   Ursula K. Le Guin

1978   *Bridge to Terabithia,*   Katherine Paterson, illus. Donna Diamond
        Come to the Edge,   Julia Cunningham
        Dear Bill, Remember Me? and Other Stories,   Norma Fox Mazer
        Manya's Story,   Bettyanne Gray
        Mischling, Second Degree: My Childhood in Nazi Germany,   Ilse Koehn
        Mr. Yowder and the Giant Bull Snake,   Glen Rounds
        Noah's Ark,   Peter Spier
        The No-Return Trail,   Sonia Levitin

Stevie, John Steptoe
Sylvester and the Magic Pebble, William Steig
Tuck Everlasting, Natalie Babbit
Who's in Rabbit's House?: A Masai Tale, Verna Aardema, illus. Leo Dillon and Diane Dillon

1977 *Abel's Island,* William Steig
Sailing to Cythera and Other Anatole Stories, Nancy Willard, illus. David McPhail
Slake's Limbo, Felice Holman

1976 *The Day the Circus Came to Lone Tree,* Glen Rounds
Don't Take Teddy, Babbis Friis-Baastad, trans. Lise Somme McKinnon
Duffy and the Devil, Harve Zemach, illus. Margot Zemach
M.C. Higgins, the Great, Virginia Hamilton
Saturday, the Twelfth of October, Norma Fox Mazer

1975 *Dust of the Earth,* Bill Cleaver and Vera Cleaver
A Hero Ain't Nothin' but a Sandwich, Alice Childress
The Pig-tale, Lewis Carroll, illus. Leonard B. Lubin

1974 No awards

1973 *Anansi the Spider: A Tale from the Ashanti,* Gerald McDermott
Cockleburr Quarters, Charlotte Baker, illus. Robert Owens
Four Women in a Violent Time, Deborah Crawford
The Girl Who Loved the Wind, Jane Yolen
Jack Tar, Jean Russell Larson, illus. Mercer Mayer
The Knee-High Man, and Other Tales, Julius Lester, illus. Ralph Pinto
Little Tim and the Brave Sea Captain, Edward Ardizzone
North to Freedom, Anne S. Holm, trans. L.W. Kingsland
Pippi Longstocking, Astrid Lindgren, trans. Florence Lamborn, illus. Louis Glanzman
The Runaway's Diary, Marilyn Harris
The Silver Pony, Lynd Ward

Snow White and the Seven Dwarfs, Jacob Grimm and Wilhelm Grimm, trans. Randall Jarrell, illus. Nancy Ekholm Burkert

The Stolen Pony, Glen Rounds

1972 *The Art and Industry of Sandcastles,* Jan Adkins

Bear Circus, William Pène du Bois

Ceremony of Innocence, James Forman

The Diary of Nina Kosterina, Nina Kosterina, illus. and trans. Mirra Ginsburg

Dorp Dead, Julia Cunningham, illus. James Spanfeller

The Duchess Bakes a Cake, Virginia Kahl

Emmet Otter's Jug-Band Christmas, Russell Hoban, illus. Lillian Hoban

The Forgotten Door, Alexander Key

The Hawkstone, Jay Williams

The Little Old Woman Who Used Her Head, Hope Newell, illus. Margaret Ruse

Long Journey Home: Stories from Black History, Julius Lester

Mrs. Frisby and the Rats of NIMH, Robert C. O'Brien, illus. Zena Bernstein

The Planet of Junior Brown, Virginia Hamilton

Simon Boom Gives a Wedding, Yuri Suhl, illus. Margot Zemach

1971 *Boy Alone,* Reginald Ottley, illus. Clyde Pearson

Down, Down the Mountain, Ellis Credle

The Endless Steppe: Growing Up in Siberia, Esther Hautzig

Farmer Hoo and the Baboons, Ida Chittum, illus. Glen Rounds

The Incredible Journey: A Tale of Three Animals, Sheila Every Burnford, illus. Carl Burger

Journey Outside, Mary Q. Steele, illus. Rocco Negri

Lift Every Voice and Sing: Words and Music, James Weldon Johnson and J. Rosamond Johnson, illus. Mozelle Thompson

The Nonsense Book of Riddles, Rhymes, Tongue Twisters, Puzzles and Jokes from American Folklore, Duncan Emrich, illus. Ib Spang Ohlsson

The Soul Brothers and Sister Lou, Kristin Hunter
Undine, Friedrich de la Motte Fouque, retold and ed. by Gertrude C. Schwebeil, illus. Eros Keith
The Velveteen Rabbit: or, How Toys Become Real, Margery Williams, illus. William Nicholson
The Witch's Brat, Rosemary Sutcliff, illus. Richard Lebenson

1970 *The Animal Family,* Randall Jarrell, illus. Maurice Sendak
The Cay, Theodore Taylor
The Egypt Game, Zilpha Keatley Snyder, illus. Alton Raible
The Enormous Egg, Oliver Butterworth, illus. Louis Darling
Gautama Buddha, in Life and Legend, Betty Kelen
Gone-Away Lake, Elizabeth Enright, illus. Beth Krush and Joe Krush
A Herd of Deer, Eilís Dillon, illus. Richard Kennedy
Honk the Moose, Phil Stong, illus. Kurt Wiese
The Midnight Fox, Betsy Byars, illus. Ann Grifalconi
Old Ben, Jesse Stuart, illus. Richard Cuffari
Otto of the Silver Hand, Howard Pyle
Sounder, William H. Armstrong, illus. James Barkley
The Summer I Was Lost, Phillip Viereck, illus. Ellen Viereck
To Be a Slave, Julius Lester, illus. Tom Feelings
The Tomten, Astrid Lindgren, illus. Harald Wiberg
The Weirdstone of Brisingamen and a Tale of Alderly, Alan Garner

1969 *The Children of Green Knowe,* Lucy M. Boston, illus. Peter Boston
Constance: A Story of Early Plymouth, Patricia Clapp
Edge of Two Worlds, Weyman Jones, illus. J.C. Kocsis
Little Toot, Hardie Gramatky
Little Women, Louisa May Alcott, illus. Jessie Willcox Smith
McBroom Tells the Truth, Sid Fleischman, illus. Kurt Werth
Seventeenth Summer, Maureen Daly
The Story of Comock the Eskimo, as Told to Robert Flaherty, ed. by Edmund Carpenter

The Storyteller's Pack, Frank R. Stockton, illus. Bernarda Bryson

Usha the Mouse Maiden, Mehlli Gobhai

Wild Horses of the Red Desert, Glen Rounds

1968   *The Ark,* Margot Benary-Isbert, trans. Clara Winston and Richard Winston

Drummer Hoff, Barbara Emberley, illus. Ed Emberley

Earthfasts, William Mayne

The Emperor and the Kite, Jane Yolen, illus. Ed Young

The Fiddler of High Lonesome, Brinton Turkle

From the Mixed-up Files of Mrs. Basil E. Frankweiler, E.L. Konigsburg

The Hunter I Might Have Been, George Mendoza, illus. DeWayne Dalrymple

My Father's Dragon, Ruth Stiles Gannett, illus. Ruth Chrisman Gannett

No Room: An Old Story, Rose Dobbs, illus. Fritz Eichenberg

Reflections on a Gift of Watermelon Pickle...and Other Modern Verse, Stephen Dunning, Edward Lueders, and Hugh Smith

The Wizard of Oz, L. Frank Baum, illus. W.W. Denslow

1967   *More Just So Stories* (phonodisc), Rudyard Kipling, narrated by Ed Begley

Tom Sawyer (phonodisc), Mark Twain (Samuel Clemens), narrated by Boris Karloff

1966   *Across Five Aprils,* Irene Hunt, illus. Albert J. Pucci

Banner in the Sky: The Story of a Boy and a Mountain, James Ramsey Ullman

A Child's Garden of Verses, Robert Louis Stevenson, illus. Brian Wildsmith

An Edge of the Forest, Agnes Smith, illus. Roberta Moynihan

Jed: The Story of a Yankee Soldier and a Southern Boy, Peter Burchard

Once a Mouse, Marcia Brown

Pappa Pellerin's Daughter, Maria Gripe, trans. Kersti French, illus. Harald Gripe

1965 *Bond of the Fire,* Anthony T. Fon Eisen, illus. W.T. Mars
The Cock, the Mouse and the Little Red Hen, Felicite LeFevre, illus. Tony Sarg
Joel and the Wild Goose, Helga Sandburg, illus. Thomas Daly
My Side of the Mountain, Jean Craighead George
The Nightingale, Hans Christian Andersen, trans. Eva LeGallienne, illus. Nancy Ekholm Burkert
The Pushcart War, Jean Merrill, illus. Ronni Solbert
The Return of the Twelves, Pauline Clarke, illus. Bernarda Bryson
Smoky, the Cowhorse, Will James
The Story about Ping, Marjorie Flack, illus. Kurt Wiese
The Wolves of Willoughby Chase, Joan Aiken, illus. Pat Marriott
A Wrinkle in Time, Madeleine L'Engle

1964 *A Little Princess: Being the Whole Story of Sara Crewe Now Told for the First Time,* Frances Hodgson Burnett, illus. Ethel F. Betts
Old Wind and Liu Li-San, Aline Glasgow, illus. Bernard Glasgow
Rascal: A Memoir of a Better of Era, Sterling North, illus. John Schoenherr
Rifles for Watie, Harold Keith, illus. Peter Burchard
Roller Skates, Ruth Sawyer, illus. Valenti Angelo
Roosevelt Grady, Louisa R. Shotwell, illus. Peter Burchard
Where the Wild Things Are, Maurice Sendak

1963 *Annuzza: A Girl of Romania,* Helen Seuberlich, trans. Stella Humphries, illus. Gerhard Pallasch
The Art of Ancient Egypt, Shirley Glubok, illus. Gerald Nook
The Cricket in Times Square, George Selden, illus. Garth Williams

Dwarf Long-nose, Wilhelm Hauff, trans. Doris Orgel, illus. Maurice Sendak
The Griffin and the Minor Canon, Frank R. Stockton, illus. Maurice Sendak
Invincible Louisa: The Story of the Author of Little Women, Cornelia L. Meigs
The Man Who Was Don Quixote: The Story of Miguel Cervantes, Rafaello Busoni
Moccasin Trail, Eloise Jarvis McGraw, illus. Paul Galdone
Rabbit Hill, Robert Lawson
The Reluctant Dragon, Kenneth Grahame, illus. Ernest H. Shepard
The Superlative Horse, Jean Merrill, illus. Ronni Solbert
Tom's Midnight Garden, A. Philippa Pearce, illus. Susan Einzig
Uncle Remus: His Songs and Sayings, Joel Chandler Harris, illus. A.B. Frost
The Water Babies, Charles Kingsley, illus. Harold Jones
The Wheel on the School, Meindert DeJong, illus. Maurice Sendak
The Yearling, Marjorie Kinnan Rawlings, illus. N.C. Wyeth

1962   *The Adventures of Huckleberry Finn,* Mark Twain (Samuel Clemens), illus. Donald McKay
The Dark Frigate, Charles Boardman Hawes, illus. A.L. Ripley
Daughter of the Mountains, Louise S. Rankin, illus. Kurt Wiese
Inch by Inch, Leo Lionni
The Lion, the Witch and the Wardrobe, C.S. Lewis, illus. Pauline Baynes
Paddle-to-the-Sea, Holling Clancy Holling
Padre Porko: The Gentlemanly Pig, Robert Davis, illus. Fritz Eichenberg
A Penny a Day, Walter de la Mare, illus. Paul Kennedy
The Tailor of Gloucester, Beatrix Potter

Thistle and Thyme: Tales and Legends from Scotland, Sorche Nic Leodhas, illus. Evaline Ness
Thumbelina, Hans Christian Andersen, trans. R.P. Keigwin, illus. Adrienne Adams
Winter Danger, William O. Steele, illus. Paul Galdone
The World of Christopher Robin, A.A. Milne, illus. Ernest H. Shepard

1961 *And to Think That I Saw It on Mulberry Street,* Dr. Seuss (Theodor S. Geisel)
Ben and Me, Robert Lawson
Blue Willow, Doris Gates, illus. Paul Lantz
The Door in the Wall: Story of Medieval London, Marguerite de Angeli
Grishka and the Bear, René Guillot, trans. Gwen Marsh, illus. Joan Kiddell-Monroe
Hitty, Her First Hundred Years, Rachel Field, illus. Dorothy P. Lathrop
Island of the Blue Dolphins, Scott O'Dell
The Moffats, Eleanor Estes, illus. Louis Slobodkin
Misty of Chincoteague, Marguerite Henry, illus. Wesley Dennis
A Roundabout Turn, Robert H. Charles, illus. L. Leslie Brooke
When I Was a Boy, Erich Kästner, trans. Isabel McHugh and Florence McHugh, illus. Horst Lemke

1960 *The Blind Colt,* Glen Rounds
The Borrowers, Mary Norton, illus. Beth Krush and Joe Krush
Curious George Takes a Job, H.A. Rey
Johnny Crow's Garden: A Picture Book, L. Leslie Brooke
The Jungle Book, Rudyard Kipling, illus. J.L. Kipling, W.H. Drake, and P. Frenzeny
Lavender's Blue: A Book of Nursery Rhymes, Kathleen Lines, illus. Harold Jones
The Matchlock Gun, Walter D. Edmonds, illus. Paul Lantz
Onion John, Joseph Krumgold, illus. Symeon Shimin
Young Fu of the Upper Yangtze, Elizabeth Foreman Lewis, illus. Kurt Wiese

1959   *Caddie Woodlawn,* Carol Ryrie Brink, illus. Kate Seredy
Charlotte's Web, E.B. White, illus. Garth Williams
The Courage of Sarah Noble, Alice Dalgliesh, illus. Leonard
Weisgard
The Five Chinese Brothers, Claire Huchet Bishop, illus. Kurt
Wiese
Li Lun, Lad of Courage, Carolyn Treffinger, illus. Kurt Wiese
The Little House, Virginia Lee Burton
The Minnow Leads to Treasure, A. Philippa Pearce, illus.
Edward Ardizzone
The Secret Garden, Frances Hodgson Burnett, illus. Nora S.
Unwin
Snipp, Snapp, Snurr and the Red Shoes, Maj Lindman
The Story of Babar, the Little Elephant, Jean de Brunhoff,
trans. Merle S. Haas
This Boy Cody, Leon Wilson, illus. Ursula Koering
Tirra Lirra: Rhymes Old and New, Laura Richards, illus.
Marguerite Davis
The White Stag, Kate Seredy

1958   *The Blue Cat of Castle Town,* Catherine C. Coblentz, illus.
Janice Holland
*Caps for Sale: A Tale of a Peddler, Some Monkeys, and Their
Monkey Business,* Esphyr Slobodkina
Horton Hatches the Egg, Dr. Seuss (Theodor S. Geisel)
*The Little Bookroom: Eleanor Farjeon's Short Stories for
Children Chosen by Herself,* Eleanor Farjeon, illus. Edward
Ardizzone
The Little Engine That Could, Watty Piper, illus. George
Hauman and Doris Hauman
The Little House in the Big Woods, Laura Ingalls Wilder, illus.
Garth Williams
Millions of Cats, Wanda Gág
Mr. Popper's Penguins, Richard Atwater and Florence Atwater,
illus. Robert Lawson
Ol' Paul, the Mighty Logger, Glen Rounds

Pecos Bill, the Greatest Cowboy of All Time, James Cloyd
Bowman, illus. Laura Bannon
Prayer for a Child, Rachel Field, illus. Elizabeth Orton Jones
The Story of Doctor Doolittle, Hugh Lofting
The Tale of Peter Rabbit, Beatrix Potter
The Three Hundred and Ninety-seventh White Elephant, René
Guillot, trans. Gwen March, illus. Moyra Leatham
The Wind in the Willows, Kenneth Grahame, illus. Ernest H.
Shepard
The World of Pooh, A.A. Milne, illus. Ernest H. Shepard

Christopher Award

੨ค

Lofty values of the human spirit, such as honor and charity, are featured in books that win this award. A bronze medallion has been given annually since 1970, emblazoned with the Christian organization's motto: "Better to light one candle than to curse the darkness." There are awards for books appealing to several age groups.

1996   *The Christmas Miracle of Jonathan Toomey,* Susan
       Wojciechowski, illus. P.J. Lynch (Ages 6–9)
       Been to Yesterdays: Poems of a Life, Lee Bennett Hopkins, illus.
       Charlene Rendeiro (Ages 10–12)
       Mother Jones: One Woman's Fight for Labor, Betsy Harvey
       Kraft (Ages 12–14)
       Parallel Journeys, Eleanor Ayer, with Helen Waterford and
       Alfons Heck (Young Adult)

1995   *I'll See You When the Moon Is Full,* Susi Gregg Fowler, illus.
       Jim Fowler (Ages 4–6)
       Prize in the Snow, Bill Easterling, illus. Mary Beth Owens
       (Ages 6–8)
       The Ledgerbook of Thomas Blue Eagle, Jewel H. Grutman and
       Gay Matthaei, illus. Adam Cvijanovic (Ages 8–12)
       Taking Hold: My Journey into Blindness, Sally Hobart
       Alexander (Ages 12 and up)

1994   *The Crystal Ball,* Gerda Marie Scheidl, illus. Nathalie
       Duroussy, trans. Rosemary Lanning (Ages 5–8)
       *It's Our World, Too! Stories of Young People Who Are Making A
       Difference,* Phillip Hoose (Ages 10 and up)
       Anne Frank: Beyond the Diary, Ruud van der Rol and Rian
       Verhoeven, trans. Tony Langham and Plym Peters (Young
       Adult)

1993   *The Rainbow Fish,* Marcus Pfister, trans. J. Alison James (Ages 5–8)
Rosie & the Yellow Ribbon, Paula DePaolo, illus. Janet Wolf (Ages 6–8)
Letters from Rifka, Karen Hesse (Ages 8–12)
Mississippi Challenge, Mildred Pitts Walter (Ages 12 and up)

1992   *Somebody Loves You, Mr. Hatch,* Eileen Spinelli, illus. Paul Yalowitz (Ages 4–6)
Stephen's Feast, Jean Richardson, illus. Alice Englander (Ages 6–8)
The Gold Coin, Alma Flor Ada, trans. Bernice Randall, illus. Neil Waldman, (Ages 8–10)
The Star Fisher, Laurence Yep (Ages 10 and up)
Where Does God Live? Questions and Answers for Parents and Children, Rabbi Marc Gellman and Monsignor Thomas Hartman, illus. William Zdinak (All Ages)

1991   *Mississippi Bridge,* Mildred D. Taylor, illus. Max Ginsburg (Ages 9–12)
Paul Revere's Ride, Henry Wadsworth Longfellow, illus. Ted Rand (All ages)

1990   *Keeping a Christmas Secret,* Phyllis Reynolds Naylor, illus. Lena Shiffman (Ages 4–7)
William and Grandpa, Alice Schertle, illus. Lydia Dabcovich (Ages 8–11)
Can the Whales Be Saved?, Dr. Phillip Whitfield (Ages 10–12)
So Much to Tell You..., John Marsden (Young Adult)

1989   *The Good-Bye Book,* Judith Viorst, illus. Kay Chorao (Ages 5–7)
Family Farm, Thomas Locker (Ages 7–10)
Lies, Deception, and Truth, Ann E. Weiss (Ages 10–14)
Looking the Tiger in the Eye: Confronting the Nuclear Threat, Carl B. Feldbaum and Ronald J. Bee (Young Adult)

1988 *Heckedy Peg,* Audrey Wood, illus. Don Wood (Picture Book)
Humphrey's Bear, Jan Wahl, illus. William Joyce (Ages 6–8)
The Gold Cadillac, Mildred D. Taylor, illus. Michael Hays
(Ages 9–12)
*Into a Strange Land: Unaccompanied Refugee Youth in
America,* Brent K. Ashabranner and Melissa Ashabranner
(Ages 12 and up)

1987 *Duncan & Delores,* Barbara Samuels (Ages 4–6)
The Purple Coat, Amy Hest, illus. Amy Schwartz (Ages 6–8)
Borrowed Summer, Marion Walker Doren (Ages 8–12)
Class Dismissed: More High School Poems, No. II, Mel Glenn,
illus. Michael J. Bernstein (Young Adult)

1986 *The Patchwork Quilt,* Valerie Flournoy, illus. Jerry Pinkney
(Ages 4–8)
Sarah, Plain and Tall, Patricia MacLachlan (Ages 8–10)
Promise Not to Tell, Carolyn Polese, illus. Jennifer Barrett
(Ages 8 and up)
Underdog, Marilyn Sachs (Ages 10–12)
The Mount Rushmore Story, Judith St. George (Young Adult)

1985 *Picnic,* Emily Arnold McCully (Picture Book)
How My Parents Learned to Eat, Ina Friedman, illus. Allen
Say (Ages 6–8)
Secrets of a Small Brother, Richard J. Margolis, illus. Donald
Carrick (Ages 8–10)
One-Eyed Cat, Paula Fox (Ages 10 and up)
Imagine That! Exploring Make Believe, Joyce Strauss, illus.
Jennifer Barrett (All ages)

1984 *Posy,* Charlotte Pomerantz, illus. Catherine Stock (Picture
Book)
Dear Mr. Henshaw, Beverly Cleary, illus. Paul O. Zelinsky
(Ages 8–10)
The Sign of the Beaver, Elizabeth George Speare (Ages 10–12)
The Nuclear Arms Race: Can We Survive It?, Ann E. Weiss
(Ages 12 and up)

1983   *We Can't Sleep,* James Stevenson (Ages 4–7)
       Homesick: My Own Story, Jean Fritz, illus. Margot Tomes
       (Ages 8–12)
       A Formal Feeling, Zibby Oneal (Ages 12 and up)
       Drawing from Nature, Jim Arnosky (All ages)

1982   *My Mom Travels a Lot,* Caroline Feller Bauer, illus. Nancy
       Winslow Parker (Picture Book)
       Even If I Did Something Awful, Barbara S. Hazen, illus. Nancy
       Kincade (Ages 6–9)
       A Gift of Mirrorvax, Malcolm MacCloud (Ages 10–14)
       The Islanders, John Rowe Townsend (Young Adult)

1981   *People,* Peter Spier (Picture Book)
       Son for a Day, Corrine Gerson, illus. Velma Ilsley (Ages 8–12)
       All Times, All Peoples: A World History of Slavery, Milton
       Meltzer, illus. Leonard Everett Fisher (Ages 8–12)
       Encounter at Easton, Avi (Ages 12 and up)
       *The Hardest Lesson: Personal Stories of a School Desegregation
       Crisis,* Pamela Bullard and Judith Stoia (Ages 12 and up)

1980   *Frederick's Alligators,* Esther Allen Peterson, illus. Susanna
       Natti
       What Happened in Hamelin?, Gloria Skurzynski (Ages 9–12)
       All Together Now, Sue Ellen Bridgers (Ages 12 and up)
       *The New York Kid's Book: 170 Children's Writers and Artists
       Celebrate New York City,* Catherine Edmonds and others
       (All ages)

1979   *Panda Cake,* Rosalie Seidler (Picture Book)
       Chester Chipmunk's Thanksgiving, Barbara Williams,
       illus. Kay Chorao (Ages 7-9)
       The Great Gilly Hopkins, Katherine Paterson (Age 9–12)
       Gentlehands, M.E. Kerr (Young Adult)

1978   *Noah's Ark,* Peter Spier (Picture Book)
       The Seeing Stick, Jane Yolen, illus. Remy Charlip and Demetra
       Marsalis (Ages 6-9)

Come to the Edge, Julia Cunningham (Ages 12 and up)
Where's Your Head? Psychology for Teenagers, Dale Bick Carlson, illus. Carol Nicklaus (Ages 12 and up)
The Wheel of King Asoka, Ashok Davar (All Ages)

1977 *Willy Bear,* Mildred Kantrowitz, illus. Nancy Winslow Parker (Picture Book)
Frog and Toad All Year, Arnold Lobel (Ages 6–8)
The Champion of Merrimack County, Roger W. Drury, illus. Fritz Wegner (Ages 9–12)
Hurry, Hurry, Mary Dear! and Other Nonsense Poems, N.M. Bodecker (Ages 9 and up)
Dear Bill, Remember Me? and Other Stories, Norma Fox Mazer (Ages 12 and up)

1976 *Anno's Alphabet: An Adventure in Imagination,* Mitsumasa Anno (Picture Book)
How the Witch Got Alf, Cora Annett Scott, illus. Steven Kellogg (Ages 7–11)
Tuck Everlasting, Natalie Babbit (Ages 9–12)
Bert Breen's Barn, Walter D. Edmonds (Ages 12 and up)
Pyramid, David Macaulay (Ages 12 and up)

1975 *Dawn,* Uri Shulevitz (Preschool)
My Grandson Lew, Charlotte Zolotow, illus. William Pène du Bois (Ages 4–8)
First Snow, Helen Coutant, illus.Vo-Dinh (Ages 8–12)
Save the Mustangs! How a Federal Law Is Passed, Ann E. Weiss (Ages 8–12)
A Billion for Boris, Mary Rodgers (Ages 12 and up)

1974 *It's Raining, Said John Twaining: Danish Nursery Rhymes,* N.M. Bodecker (Preschool)
Gorilla, Gorilla, Carol Fenner, illus. by Symeon Shimin (Ages 4–8)
I'll Protect You from the Jungle Beasts, Martha Alexander (Ages 4–8)

The Wolf, Michael Fox, illus. Charles Frace (Ages 8–12)
Guests in the Promised Land: Stories, Kristin Hunter (Ages 12 and up)
The Right to Know: Censorship in America, Robert A. Liston (Ages 12 and up)

1973 *The Adventures of Obadiah,* Brinton Turkle (Ages 4–8)
The Book of Giant Stories, David L. Harrison, illus.Philippe Fix (Ages 8–12)
Tracking the Unearthly Creatures of Marsh and Pond, Howard G. Smith, illus. Anne Marie Jauss (Ages 8–12)
Freaky Friday, Mary Rodgers (Teenage)
Vanishing Wings: A Tale of Three Birds of Prey, Griffing Bancroft, illus. John Hamberger (Teenage)
This Star Shall Abide, Sylvia Louise Engdahl, illus. Richard Cuffari (Young Adult)
Dominic, William Steig (All ages)

1972 *Emmet Otter's Jug-Band Christmas,* Russell Hoban, illus. Lillian Hoban (Ages 4–8)
On the Day Peter Stuyvesant Sailed into Town, Arnold Lobel (Ages 4–8)
Annie and the Old One, Miska Miles, illus. Peter Parnall (Ages 8–12)
Pocahontas and the Strangers, Clyde Robert Bulla, illus. Peter Burchard (Ages 8–12)
The Headless Cupid, Zilpha Keatley Snyder, illus. Alton Raible (Teenage)
The Rights of the People: The Major Decisions of the Warren Court, Walter Goodman and Elaine Goodman (Teenage)

1971 *The Erie Canal,* Peter Spier (Ages 4–8)
A Moment of Silence, Pierre Janssen, trans. William R. Tyler, illus. Hans Samson (Ages 8–12)
The Changeling, Zilpha Keatley Snyder, illus. Alton Raible (Ages 8–12)
The Guardians, John Christopher (Teenage)

Sea and Earth: The Life of Rachel Carson, Philip Sterling (Teenage)

UNICEF Book of Children's Legends; UNICEF Book of Children's Poems; UNICEF Book of Children's Prayers; and *UNICEF Book of Children's Songs,* William I. Kaufman (All ages)

1970   *Alexander and the Wind-up Mouse,* Leo Lionni (Ages 4–8)

Tucker's Countryside, George Selden, illus. Garth Williams (Ages 8–12)

Brother, Can You Spare a Dime? The Great Depression, 1929–1933, Milton Meltzer (Teenage)

Escape from Nowhere, Jeanette Eyerly (Teenage)

Edgar Allan Poe Award

ès

The "Edgar" honors great suspense, detective, and spy works. There are two awards for young audiences. Named for the writer of such chilling stories and poetry as "The Tell-Tale Heart" and "The Raven," the juvenile award was first granted in 1954, followed by that for young adults in 1989. Judges are members of the Mystery Writers of America. The winners are presented with a ceramic bust of Poe at the Mystery Writer's spring convention.

Juvenile

1996   *Prophecy Rock*, Rob MacGregor

1995   *The Absolutely True Story...How I Visited Yellowstone Park with the Terrible Rupes*, Willo Davis Roberts

1994   *The Twin in the Tavern*, Barbara Brooks Wallace

1993   *Coffin on a Case*, Eve Bunting

1992   *Wanted...Mud Blossom*, Betsy Byars

1991   *Stonewords: A Ghost Story*, Pam Conrad

1990   No award

1989   *Megan's Island*, Willo Davis Roberts

1988   *Lucy Forever and Miss Rosetree, Shrinks*, Susan Shreve

1987   *The Other Side of Dark*, Joan Lowery Nixon

1986   *The Sandman's Eyes*, Patricia Windsor

1985   *Night Cry*, Phyllis Reynolds Naylor

1984   *The Callender Papers*, Cynthia Voigt

1983   *The Murder of Hound Dog Bates: A Novel*, Robbie Branscum

1982   *Taking Terri Mueller*, Norma Fox Mazer

1981   *The Seance,* Joan Lowery Nixon

1980   *The Kidnapping of Christina Lattimore,* Joan Lowery Nixon

1979   *Alone in Wolf Hollow,* Dana Brookins

1978   *A Really Weird Summer,* Eloise Jarvis McGraw

1977   *Are You in the House Alone?,* Richard Peck

1976   *Z for Zachariah,* Robert C. O'Brien

1975   *The Dangling Witness: A Mystery,* Jay Bennett

1974   *The Long Black Coat,* Jay Bennett

1973   *Deathwatch,* Robb White

1972   *Night Fall,* Joan Aiken

1971   *The Intruder,* John Rowe Townsend, illus. Joseph A. Phelan

1970   *Danger at Black Dyke,* Winifred Finlay

1969   *The House of Dies Drear,* Virginia Hamilton, illus. Eros Keith

1968   *Signpost to Terror,* Gretchen Sprague

1967   *Sinbad and Me,* Kin Platt

1966   *The Mystery of 22 East,* Leon Ware

1965   *The Mystery at Crane's Landing,* Marcella Thum

1964   *The Mystery of the Hidden Hand,* Phyllis A. Whitney, illus. H. Tom Hall

1963   *Cutlass Island,* Scott Corbett, illus. Leonard Shortall

1962   *The Phantom of Walkaway Hill,* Edward Fenton, illus. Jo Ann Stover

1961   *The Mystery of the Haunted Pool,* Phyllis A. Whitney, illus. H. Tom Hall

Young Adult

1996 *Looking for Jamie Bridger,* Nancy Springer

1995 *Toughing It,* Nancy Springer

1994 *The Name of the Game Was Murder,* Joan Lowery Nixon

1993 *A Little Bit Dead,* Chap Reaver

1992 *The Weirdo,* Ted Taylor

1991 *Mote,* Chap Reaver

1990 *Show Me the Evidence,* Alane Ferguson

1989 *Incident at Loring Groves,* Sonia Levitin

Dorothy Canfield Fisher Children's Book Award

૨૪

The belief that good books are preventive medicine for juvenile delinquency stimulated librarians and teachers in Vermont to establish this award in 1958. Middle-school children themselves, ages 8 to 13, choose their favorites from a list of 30 fiction and nonfiction titles compiled by adults. The award is named for a well-loved Vermont resident, author of *Understood Betsy*. Voters look for originality and sound moral values. Winners are announced in May.

1995 *The Boggart*, Susan Cooper

1994 *Jennifer Murdley's Toad*, Bruce Coville

1993 *Shiloh*, Phyllis Reynolds Naylor

1992 *Maniac Magee*, Jerry Spinelli

1991 *Number the Stars*, Lois Lowry

1990 *Where It Stops, Nobody Knows*, Amy Ehrlich

1989 *Hatchet*, Gary Paulsen

1988 *Wait Till Helen Comes: A Ghost Story*, Mary Downing Hahn

1987 *The Castle in the Attic*, Elizabeth Winthrop, illus. Trina Schart Hyman

1986 *The War with Grandpa*, Robert Kimmel Smith, illus. Richard Lauter

1985 *Dear Mr. Henshaw*, Beverly Cleary, illus. Paul O. Zelinsky

1984 *A Bundle of Sticks*, Pat Rhoads Mauser, illus. Gail Owens

1983 *Tiger Eyes*, Judy Blume

1982 *The Hand-Me-Down Kid,* Francine Pascal

1981 *Bunnicula: A Rabbit-Tale of Mystery,* Deborah Howe and James Howe, illus. Alan Daniel

1980 *Bones on Black Spruce Mountain,* David Budbill

1979 *Kid Power,* Susan Beth Pfeffer, illus. Leigh Grant

1978 *Summer of Fear,* Lois Duncan

1977 *A Smart Kid Like You,* Stella Pevsner

1976 *The Toothpaste Millionaire,* Jean Merrill, illus. Jan Palmer

1975 *The Eighteenth Emergency,* Betsy Byars, illus. Robert Grossman

1974 *Catch a Killer,* George A. Woods

1973 *Never Steal a Magic Cat,* Don Caufield and Joan Caufield, illus. Jan Palmer

1972 *Flight of the White Wolf,* Mel Ellis

1971 *Go to the Room of the Eyes,* Betty K. Erwin, illus. Irene Burns

1970 *Kavik the Wolf Dog,* Walt Morey, illus. Peter Parnall

1969 *Two in the Wilderness,* Mary W. Thompson, illus. Tom O'Sullivan

1968 *The Taste of Spruce Gum,* Jacqueline Jackson, illus. Lilian Obligado

1967 *The Summer I Was Lost,* Phillip Viereck, illus. Ellen Viereck

1966 *Ribsy,* Beverly Cleary, illus. Louis Darling

1965 *Rascal: A Memoir of a Better Era,* Sterling North, illus. John Schoenherr

1964 *Bristle Face,* Zachary Ball

1963 *The Incredible Journey: A Tale of Three Animals,* Sheila Every Burnford, illus. Carl Burger

1962 *The City under the Back Steps,* Evelyn Lampman, illus. Honore Valintcourt

1961 *Captain Ghost,* Thelma H. Bell, illus. Corydon Bell

1960 *Double or Nothing,* Phoebe Erickson

1959 *Commanche of the Seventh,* Margaret C. Leighton, illus. Elliott Means

1958 *Fifteen,* Beverly Cleary, illus. Joe Krush and Beth Krush

1957 *Old Bones, the Wonder Horse,* Mildred M. Pace, illus. Wesley Dennis

Golden Kite Award

ۿ

Writers and illustrators themselves vote for the best work of their peers. The well-respected Society of Children's Book Writers and Illustrators has expanded its mission over the years to applaud books of nonfiction and illustration as well as fiction. The winner is a society member who has created a book that best addresses the fascinations and concerns of children. A statuette is awarded each spring.

Fiction

1995 *The Watsons Go to Birmingham—1963*, Christopher Paul Curtis

1994 *Catherine, Called Birdy*, Karen Cushman

1993 *Make Lemonade*, Virginia Euwer Wolff

1992 *Letters from a Slave Girl: The Story of Harriet Jacobs*, Mary E. Lyons

1991 *The Raincatchers*, Jean Thesman

1990 *The True Confessions of Charlotte Doyle*, Avi, illus. Ruth E. Murray

1989 *Jenny of the Tetons*, Kristiana Gregory

1988 *Borrowed Children*, George Ella Lyon

1987 *Rabble Starkey*, Lois Lowry

1986 *After the Dancing Days*, Margaret Rostkowski

1985 *Sarah, Plain and Tall*, Patricia MacLachlan

1984 *Tancy*, Belinda Hurmence

1983 *The Tempering*, Gloria Skurzynski

1982 *Ralph S. Mouse*, Beverly Cleary, illus. Paul O. Zelinsky

1981 *Little, Little*, M.E. Kerr

1980 *Arthur, for the Very First Time,* Patricia MacLachlan, illus. Lloyd Bloom

1979 *The Magic of the Glits,* Carole S. Adler, illus. Ati Forberg

1978 *And You Give Me a Pain, Elaine,* Stella Pevsner

1977 *The Girl Who Had No Name,* Bernice Rabe

1976 *One More Flight,* Eve Bunting, illus. Diane de Groat

1975 *The Garden Is Doing Fine,* Carol Farley, illus. Lynn Sweat

1974 *The Girl Who Cried Flowers and Other Tales,* Jane Yolen, illus. David Palladini

1973 *Summer of My German Soldier,* Bette Green

Nonfiction

1995 *Abigail Adams: Witness to a Revolution,* Natalie S. Bober

1994 *Kids at Work: Lewis Hine and the Crusade Against Child Labor,* Russell Freedman

1993 *Eleanor Roosevelt: A Life of Discovery,* Russell Freedman

1992 *The Long Road to Gettysburg,* Jim Murphy

1991 *The Wright Brothers: How They Invented the Airplane,* Russell Freedman

1990 *The Boy's War,* Jim Murphy

1989 *Panama Canal: Gateway to the World,* Judith St. George

1988 *Let There Be Light,* James Cross Giblin

1987 *The Incredible Journey of Lewis and Clark,* Rhoda Blumberg

1986 *Poverty in America,* Milton Meltzer

1985 *Commodore Perry in the Land of the Shogun,* Rhoda Blumberg

1984 *Walls: Defenses Throughout History,* James Cross Giblin

1983 *The Illustrated Dinosaur Dictionary,* Helen Roney Sattler

1982 *Chimney Sweeps,* James Cross Giblin, illus. Margot Tomes

1981 *Blissymbolics: Speaking Without Speech,* Elizabeth S. Helfman

1980 *The Lives of Spiders,* Dorothy Hinshaw Patent

1979 *Runaway Teens,* Arnold Madison

1978 *How I Came to Be a Writer,* Phyllis Reynolds Naylor

1977 *Peeper, First Voice of Spring,* Robert McClung, illus. Carol Lerner

Illustration

1995 *Fairy Wings,* Lauren Mills, illus. Lauren Mills and Dennis Nolan

1994 *Big Fat Hen,* Keith Baker

1993 *By the Light of the Halloween Moon,* Kevin Hawkes

1992 *Chicken Sunday,* Patricia Polacco

1991 *Mama, Do You Love Me?,* Barbara M. Joose, illus. Barbara Lavallee

1990 *Home Place,* Crescent Dragonwagon, illus. Jerry Pinkney

1989 *Tom Thumb,* Richard Jesse Watson

1988 *Forest of Dreams,* Rosemary Wells, illus. Susan Jeffers

1987 *The Devil & Mother Crump,* Valerie Scho Carey, illus. Arnold Lobel

1986 *Alphabatics,* Suse MacDonald

1985 *The Donkey's Dream,* Barbara Helen Berger

1984 *The Napping House,* Audrey Wood, illus. Don Wood

1983 *Little Red Riding Hood,* Jacob Grimm and Wilhelm Grimm, retold by and illus. Trina Schart Hyman

1982 *Giorgio's Village,* Tomie dePaola

Governor General's Literary Award

೭೩

Canadian writers and illustrators collect $10,000 by winning this prize. Sponsored by the writing and publishing section of The Canada Council, this series of awards also includes French-language books. Only English-language titles are featured here.

Author

1995   *The Maestro,* Tim Wynne-Jones

1994   *Adam and Eve and Pinch-Me,* Julie Johnston

1993   *Some of the Kinder Planets,* Tim Wynne-Jones

1992   *Hero of Lesser Causes,* Julie Johnston

1991   *Pick-up Sticks,* Sarah Ellis

1990   *Redwork,* Michael Bedard

1989   *Bad Boy,* Diana Wieler

1988   *The Third Magic,* Welwyn Wilton Katz

1987   *Galahad Schwartz and the Cockroach Army,* Morgan Nyberg

1986   *Shadow in Hawthorn Bay,* Janet Lunn

1985   *Julie,* Cora Taylor

1984   *Sweetgrass,* Jan Hudson

1983   *The Ghost Horse of the Mounties,* Sean O. Huigin

1982   *Hunter in the Dark,* Monica Hughes

1981   *The Guardian of Isis,* Monica Hughes

1980   *The Trouble with Princesses,* Christie Harris, illus. Douglas Tait

1979   *Days of Terror,* Barbara Claassen Smucker

1978   *Hold Fast,* Kevin Major

1977   *Listen for the Singing,* Jean Little

1976   *The Wooden People,* Myra Paperny, illus. Ken Stampnick

1975   *Shantymen of Cache Lake,* Bill Freeman

1959–1974   No awards

Illustrator

1995   *The Last Quest of Gilgamesh,* Ludmilla Zeman

1994   *Josepha: A Prairie Boy's Story,* Jim McGugan, illus. Murray Kimber

1993   *Sleep Tight, Mrs. Ming,* Sharon Jennings, illus. Mireille Levert

1992   *Waiting for the Whales,* Sheryl McFarlane, illus. Ron Lightburn

1991   *Doctor Kiss Says Yes,* Teddy Jam, illus. Joanne Fitzgerald

1990   *The Orphan Boy,* Tololwa M. Mollel, illus. Paul Morin

1989   *The Magic Paintbrush,* Robin Muller

1988   *Amos's Sweater,* Janet Lunn, illus. Kim LaFave

1987   *Rainy Day Magic,* Marie-Louise Gay

1986   *Have You Seen Birds?,* Joanne Oppenheim, illus. Barbara Reid

1985   *Murdo's Story: A Legend from Northern Manitoba,* Murdo Scribe, illus. Terry Gallagher

1984   *Lizzy's Lion,* Dennis Lee, illus. Marie-Louise Gay

1983   *The Little Mermaid,* Hans Christian Andersen, retold by Margaret Crawford Maloney, illus. László Gál

1982   *ABC, 123: The Canadian Alphabet and Counting Book,* Vlasta van Kampen

1981 *Ytek and the Arctic Orchid: An Inuit Legend,* Garnet Hewitt, illus. Heather Woodall

1980 *Petrouchka,* Elizabeth Cleaver

1979 *The Twelve Dancing Princesses: A Fairy Tale,* retold by Janet Lunn, illus. László Gál

1978 *A Salmon for Simon,* Betty Waterton, illus. Ann Blades

1959-1977 No awards

Early Winners

1958 *Nkwala,* Edith Lambert Sharp, illus. William Winter

1957 *The Great Chief: Maskepetoon, Warrior of the Crees,* Kerry Wood, illus. John A. Hall

1956 *Lost in the Barrens,* Farley Mowat, illus. Charles Greer

1955 *The Map Maker,* Kerry Wood

1954 *The Nor'westers: The Fight for the Fur Trade,* Marjorie Wilkins Campbell, illus. Illingworth Kerr

1953 *Rebels Ride at Night,* John F. Hayes, illus. Fred J. Finley

1952 *Cargoes on the Great Lakes,* Marie McPhedran, illus. Dorothy Ivens

1951 *A Land Divided,* John F. Hayes, illus. Fred J. Finley

1950 *The Great Adventure: An Illustrated History of Canada,* Donalda Dickie, illus. Lloyd Scott

1949 *Franklin of the Arctic: A Life of Adventure,* Richard S. Lambert

Kate Greenaway Medal

≿❧

The best illustrated children's books in the United Kingdom are given this award. It is named for Kate Greenaway, the nineteenth-century English author and illustrator of such memorable works as *The Language of Flowers* and *A Day in a Child's Life*. Like the Carnegie Medal, this award is administered by the British Library Association. In addition to a medal, winners receive the right to designate over $1,000 worth of books to the organization of their choice.

1994   *Way Home,* Gregory Rogers

1993   *Black Ships Before Troy,* Alan Lee

1992   *Zoo,* Anthony Browne

1991   *The Jolly Christmas Postman,* Allan Ahlberg and Janet Ahlberg

1990   *The Whale's Song,* Dyan Sheldon, illus. Gary Blythe

1989   *War Boy: A Country Childhood,* Michael Foreman

1988   *Can't You Sleep, Little Bear?,* Martin Waddell, illus. Barbara Firth

1987   *Crafty Chameleon,* Mwenye Hadithi, illus. Adrienne Kennaway

1986   *Snow White in New York,* Fiona French

1985   *Sir Gawain and the Loathly Lady,* retold by Selina Hastings, illus. Juan Wijngaard

1984   *Hiawatha's Childhood,* Henry Wadsworth Longfellow, illus. Errol Le Cain

1983   *Gorilla,* Anthony Browne

1982   *Long Neck and Thunder Foot,* Helen Piers, illus. Michael
        Foreman
        Sleeping Beauty and Other Favourite Fairy Tales, Angela
        Carter, illus. Michael Foreman

1981   *The Highwayman,* Alfred Noyes, illus. Charles Keeping

1980   *Mr. Magnolia,* Quentin Blake

1979   *The Haunted House,* Jan Pienkowski

1978   *Each Peach Pear Plum,* Allan Ahlberg and Janet Ahlberg

1977   *Dogger,* Shirley Hughes

1976   *The Post Office Cat,* Gail E. Haley

1975   *Horses in Battle* and *Mishka,* Victor G. Ambrus

1974   *The Wind Blew,* Pat Hutchins

1973   *Father Christmas,* Raymond Briggs

1972   *The Woodcutter's Duck,* Krystyna Turska

1971   *The Kingdom under the Sea,* Jan Pienkowski

1970   *Mr. Gumpy's Outing,* John Burningham

1969   *The Dragon of an Ordinary Family,* Margaret Mahy, illus.
        Helen Oxenbury
        The Quangle Wangle's Hat, Edward Lear, illus. Helen
        Oxenbury

1968   *Dictionary of Chivalry,* Grant Uden, illus. Pauline Baynes

1967   *Charley, Charlotte, and the Golden Canary,* Charles Keeping

1966   *The Mother Goose Treasury,* Raymond Briggs

1965   *The Three Poor Tailors,* Victor G. Ambrus

1964   *Shakespeare's Theatre,* C. Walter Hodges

1963   *Borka: The Adventures of a Goose with No Feathers,* John
        Burningham

1962   *Brian Wildsmith's ABC,* Brian Wildsmith

1961   *Mrs. Cockle's Cat,* A. Philippa Pearce, illus. Antony Maitland

1960   *Old Winkle and the Seagulls,* Elizabeth Rose, illus. Gerald Rose

1959   *A Bundle of Ballads,* Ruth Manning-Sanders, illus. William Stobbs
Kashtanka, Anton Chekov, trans. Charles Dowsett, illus. William Stobbs

1958   No award

1957   *Mrs. Easter and the Storks,* V.H. Drummond

1956   *Tim All Alone,* Edward Ardizzone

Iowa Teen Award

᠍᠍᠍᠍᠍᠍᠍᠍

Teenagers in Iowa vote for recipients of this award. Winning books feature the pangs and pains of adolescence. Eager to stimulate reading in schoolchildren ages 12 to 15, the Iowa Educational Media Association also created this award as a vehicle to give young people the chance to make significant decisions and to work with adults. Winning books must have been published within three years prior to the vote.

1995   *Whatever Happened to Janie?*, Caroline B. Cooney

1994   *Ryan White, My Own Story*, Ryan White

1993   *The Face on the Milk Carton*, Caroline B. Cooney

1992   *Don't Look Behind You*, Lois Duncan

1991   *Silver*, Norma Fox Mazer

1990   *Hatchet*, Gary Paulsen

1989   *The Other Side of Dark*, Joan Lowery Nixon

1988   *Abby, My Love*, Hadley Irwin

1987   *You Shouldn't Have to Say Good-bye*, Patricia Hermes

1986   *When We First Met*, Norma Fox Mazer

1985   *Tiger Eyes*, Judy Blume

Coretta Scott King Book Award

❧

Books by African-American authors and illustrators that are particularly educational and inspirational receive this honor. Winning titles celebrate black history, spirit, and dreams in fiction and nonfiction. The award is administered by the Social Responsibilities Round Table of the American Library Association and is named for the wife of the late social activist, Dr. Martin Luther King, Jr. Mrs. King is honored for her work toward brotherhood and world peace. Award winners receive a citation, $250, and a set of encyclopedias.

Author

1996   *Her Stories: African American Folktales, Fairy Tales and True Tales,* Virginia Hamilton, illus. Leo Dillon and Diane Dillon

1995   *Christmas in the Big House, Christmas in the Quarters,* Patricia C. McKissack and Fredrick McKissack, illus. John Thompson

1994   *Toning the Sweep,* Angela Johnson

1993   *The Dark-Thirty: Southern Tales of the Supernatural,* Patricia C. McKissack

1992   *Now Is Your Time! The African American Struggle for Freedom,* Walter Dean Myers

1991   *The Road to Memphis,* Mildred D. Taylor

1990   *A Long Hard Journey: The Story of the Pullman Porter,* Patricia C. McKissack and Fredrick McKissack

1989   *Fallen Angels,* Walter Dean Myers

1988   *The Friendship,* Mildred D. Taylor, illus. Max Ginsburg

1987 *Justin and the Best Biscuits in the World,* Mildred Pitts Walter, illus. Catherine Stock

1986 *The People Could Fly: American Black Folktales,* Virginia Hamilton, illus. Leo Dillon and Diane Dillon

1985 *Motown and Didi: A Love Story,* Walter Dean Myers

1984 *Everett Anderson's Goodbye,* Lucille Clifton, illus. Ann Grifalconi

1983 *Sweet Whispers, Brother Rush,* Virginia Hamilton

1982 *Let the Circle Be Unbroken,* Mildred D. Taylor

1981 *This Life,* Sidney Poitier

1980 *The Young Landlords,* Walter Dean Myers

1979 *Escape to Freedom: A Play about Young Frederick Douglass,* Ossie Davis

1978 *Africa Dream,* Eloise Greenfield, illus. Carole Byard

1977 *The Story of Stevie Wonder,* James Haskins

1976 *Duey's Tale,* Pearl Bailey, illus. Arnold Skolnick and Gary Azon

1975 *The Legend of Africania,* Dorothy Robinson, illus. Herbert Temple

1974 *Ray Charles,* Sharon Bell Mathis, illus. George Ford

1973 *I Never Had It Made: The Autobiography of Jackie Robinson,* Jackie Robinson as told to Alfred Duckett

1972 *Seventeen Black Artists,* Elton C. Fax

1971 *Black Troubadour: Langston Hughes,* Charlemae Rollins

1970 *Dr. Martin Luther King, Jr.: Man of Peace,* Lillie Patterson, illus. Victor Mays

Illustrator

1996 *The Middle Passage: White Ships/Black Cargo,* Tom Feelings

1995 *The Creation,* James Weldon Johnson, illus. James Ransome

1994 *Soul Look Back in Wonder: Collection of African-American Poets,* ed. by Phyllis Fogelman, illus. Tom Feelings

1993 *The Origin of Life on Earth: An African Creation Myth,* retold by David A. Anderson, illus. Kathleen Atkins Wilson

1992 *Tar Beach,* Faith Ringgold

1991 *Aïda,* Leontyne Price, illus. Leo Dillon and Diane Dillon

1990 *Nathaniel Talking,* Eloise Greenfield, illus. Jan Spivey Gilchrist

1989 *Mirandy and Brother Wind,* Patricia C. McKissack, illus. Jerry Pinkney

1988 *Mufaro's Beautiful Daughters: An African Tale,* John Steptoe

1987 *Half a Moon and One Whole Star,* Crescent Dragonwagon, illus. Jerry Pinkney

1986 *The Patchwork Quilt,* Valerie Flournoy, illus. Jerry Pinkney

1985 No award

1984 *My Mama Needs Me,* Mildred Pitts Walter, illus. Pat Cummings

1983 *Black Child,* Peter Magubane

1982 *Mother Crocodile: An Uncle Amadou Tale from Senegal,* trans. Rosa Guy, illus. John Steptoe

1981 *Beat the Story-Drum, Pum-Pum,* Ashley Bryan

1980 *Cornrows,* Camille Yarbrough, illus. Carole Byard

1979 *Something on My Mind,* Nikki Grimes, illus. Tom Feelings

NCTE Award for Excellence in Poetry for Children

૨૧

Poetry is honored in this award created by the National Council for Teachers of English. The council's intention is to foster the production of high-quality poetry for younger audiences. The poetry ranges from playful to thought-provoking verse. Every three years, the NCTE chooses an American poet to honor.

1994   Barbara Juster Esbensen

1991   Valerie Worth

1988   Arnold Adoff

1985   Lilian Moore

1982   John Ciardi

1981   Eve Merriam

1980   Myra Cohn Livingston

1979   Karla Kuskin

1978   Aileen Fisher

1977   David McCord

National Jewish Book Award

❧

How does being Jewish affect a person's life? Here are two National Jewish Book awards: one for the book or collection of stories that best addresses that theme, another for picture books. Each year, the Jewish Book Council recognizes a specific book author and illustrator with a certificate and $750.

Author

1995   *Under the Domim Tree,* Gila Almagor

1994   *Golden Windows and Other Stories of Jerusalem,* Adèle Geras

1993   *Letters from Rifka,* Karen Hesse

1992   *The Man from the Other Side,* Uri Orlev, trans. Hillel Halkin

1991   *Becoming Gershona,* Nava Semel

1990   *Number the Stars,* Lois Lowry

1989   *The Devil's Arithmetic,* Jane Yolen

1988   *The Return,* Sonia Levitin

1987   *Monday in Odessa,* Eileen Bluestone Sherman

1986   *In Kindling Flame: The Story of Hannah Senesh, 1921–1944,* Linda Atkinson

1985   *Good if It Goes,* Gary Provost and Gail Levine-Freidus

1984   *The Jewish Kids Catalog,* Chaya M. Burstein

1983   *King of the Seventh Grade,* Barbara Cohen

1982   *The Night Journey,* Kathryn Lasky, illus. Trina Schart Hyman

1981 *A Russian Farewell,* Leonard Everett Fisher

1980 *Dita Saxova,* Arnošt Lustig, trans. Jeanne Nemcova

1979 *Joshua: Fighter for Bar Kochba,* Irena Narell

1978 *Never to Forget: The Jews of the Holocaust,* Milton Meltzer

1977 *Rifka Grows Up,* Chaya M. Burstein

1976 *Haym Salomon: Liberty's Son,* Shirley G. Milgrim, illus. Richard Fish

1975 *The Holocaust: A History of Courage and Resistance,* Bea Stadtler, illus. David Stone Martin

1974 *Uncle Misha's Partisans,* Yuri Suhl

1973 *The Upstairs Room,* Johanna Reiss

1972 *The Master of Miracle: A New Novel of the Golem,* Sulamith Ish-Kishor, illus. Arnold Lobel

1971 *Journey to America,* Sonia Levitin, illus. Charles Robinson

1970 *Martin Buber: Wisdom in Our Time,* Charlie May Simon
     The Story of Masada, Yigael Yadin, retold by Gerald Gottlieb

1968–1969 No award

1967 *The Story of Israel,* Meyer Levin, illus. Eli Levin

1966 *The Dreyfus Affair,* Betty Schechter

1965 *Worlds Lost and Found,* Dov Peretz Elkins and Azriel Eisenberg, illus. Charles Pickard

1964 *A Boy of Old Prague,* Sulamith Ish-Kishor, illus. Ben Shahn

1963 *Return to Freedom,* Josephine Kamm, illus. William Stobbs

1962 *Ten and a Kid,* Sadie Rose Weilerstein, illus. Janina Domanaska

1961 *Discovering Israel,* Regina Tor

1960 *Keys to a Magic Door: Isaac Leib Peretz,* Sylvia Rothchild, illus. Bernard Krigstein

1959 *Border Hawk: August Bondi,* Lloyd Alexander, illus. Bernard Krigstein

1958 *Junior Jewish Encyclopedia,* Naomi Ben-Asher and Hayim Leaf

1957 Elma E. Levinger (for body of work)

1956 Sadie Rose Weilerstein (for body of work)

1955 *King Solomon's Navy,* Nora Benjamin Kubie

1954 *The Jewish People: Book Three,* Deborah Pessin, illus. Ruth Levin

1953 *Star Light Stories: Holiday and Sabbath Tales,* Lillian Simon Freehof, illus. Jessie B. Robinson
Stories of King David, Lillian Simon Freehof, illus. Seymour R. Kaplan

1952 *All-of-a-Kind Family,* Sydney Taylor, illus. Helen John

Illustrator

1995 No award

1994 *The Always Prayer Shawl,* Sheldon Oberman, illus. Ted Lewin

1993 *Elijah's Angel: A Story for Chanukah and Christmas,* Michael J. Rosen, illus. Aminah Brenda Lynn Robinson

1992 *Chicken Man,* Michelle Edwards

1991 *Hanukkah!,* Roni Schotter, illus. Marylin Hafner

1990 *Berchick,* Esther Silverstein Blanc, illus. Tennessee Dixon

1989 *Just Enough Is Plenty: A Hanukkah Tale,* Barbara Diamond Goldin, illus. Seymour Chwast

1988   *Exodus,* adapted from the Bible by Miriam Chaikin, illus.
        Charles Mikolaycak

1987   *Poems for Jewish Holidays,* Myra Cohn Livingston, illus. Lloyd
        Bloom

1986   *Brothers,* retold by Florence B. Freedman, illus. Robert
        Andrew Parker

1985   *Mrs. Moskowitz and the Sabbath Candlesticks,* Amy Schwartz

1984   No award

1983   *Yussel's Prayer: A Yom Kippur Story,* Barbara Cohen, illus.
        Michael J. Deraney

Newbery Medal

The best American children's literature is granted this well-known distinction. Like the Caldecott Medal, this children's book award is administered by the American Library Association. It is named for the eighteenth-century Englishman John Newbery, who was the first publisher and seller of children's books. Starting in 1922, a medal has been awarded each February.

1996   *The Midwife's Apprentice,* Karen Cushman

1995   *Walk Two Moons,* Sharon Creech

1994   *The Giver,* Lois Lowry

1993   *Missing May,* Cynthia Rylant

1992   *Shiloh,* Phyllis Reynolds Naylor

1991   *Maniac Magee,* Jerry Spinelli

1990   *Number the Stars,* Lois Lowry

1989   *Joyful Noise: Poems for Two Voices,* Paul Fleischman, illus. Eric Beddows

1988   *Lincoln: A Photobiography,* Russell Freedman

1987   *The Whipping Boy,* Sid Fleischman, illus. Peter Sis

1986   *Sarah, Plain and Tall,* Patricia MacLachlan

1985   *The Hero and the Crown,* Robin McKinley

1984   *Dear Mr. Henshaw,* Beverly Cleary, illus. Paul O. Zelinsky

1983   *Dicey's Song,* Cynthia Voigt

1982   *A Visit to William Blake's Inn: Poems for Innocent and Experienced Travelers,* Nancy Willard, illus. Alice Provensen and Martin Provensen

1981   *Jacob Have I Loved,* Katherine Paterson

1980   *A Gathering of Days,* Joan W. Blos

1979   *The Westing Game,* Ellen Raskin

1978   *Bridge to Terabithia,* Katherine Paterson, illus. Donna
Diamond

1977   *Roll of Thunder, Hear My Cry,* Mildred D. Taylor, illus. Jerry
Pinkney

1976   *The Grey King,* Susan Cooper, illus. Michael Heslop

1975   *M.C. Higgins, the Great,* Virginia Hamilton

1974   *The Slave Dancer,* Paula Fox, illus. Eros Keith

1973   *Julie of the Wolves,* Jean Craighead George, illus. John
Schoenherr

1972   *Mrs. Frisby and the Rats of NIMH,* Robert C. O'Brien, illus.
Zena Bernstein

1971   *The Summer of the Swans,* Betsy Byars, illus. Ted CoConis

1970   *Sounder,* William H. Armstrong, illus. James Barkley

1969   *The High King,* Lloyd Alexander

1968   *From the Mixed-up Files of Mrs. Basil E. Frankweiler,* E.L.
Konigsburg

1967   *Up a Road Slowly,* Irene Hunt

1966   *I, Juan de Pareja,* Elizabeth Borton de Trevino

1965   *Shadow of a Bull,* Maia Wojciechowska, illus. Alvin Smith

1964   *It's Like This, Cat,* Emily Cheney Neville, illus. Emil Weiss

1963   *A Wrinkle in Time,* Madeleine L'Engle

1962   *The Bronze Bow,* Elizabeth George Speare

1961   *Island of the Blue Dolphins,* Scott O'Dell

1960 *Onion John,* Joseph Krumgold, illus. Symeon Shimin

1959 *The Witch of Blackbird Pond,* Elizabeth George Speare

1958 *Rifles for Watie,* Harold Keith, illus. Peter Burchard

1957 *Miracles on Maple Hill,* Virginia Sorensen, illus. Beth Krush and Joe Krush

1956 *Carry On, Mr. Bowditch,* Jean Lee Latham, illus. J.O. Cosgrove

1955 *The Wheel on the School,* Meindert DeJong, illus. Maurice Sendak

1954 *...And Now Miguel,* Joseph Krumgold, illus. Jean Charlot

1953 *Secret of the Andes,* Ann Nolan Clark, illus. Jean Charlot

1952 *Ginger Pye,* Eleanor Estes

1951 *Amos Fortune, Free Man,* Elizabeth Yates, illus. Nora S. Unwin

1950 *The Door in the Wall: Story of Medieval London,* Marguerite de Angeli

1949 *King of the Wind,* Marguerite Henry, illus. Wesley Dennis

1948 *The Twenty-One Balloons,* William Pène du Bois

1947 *Miss Hickory,* Carolyn Sherwin Bailey, illus. Ruth Chrisman Gannett

1946 *Strawberry Girl,* Lois Lenski

1945 *Rabbit Hill,* Robert Lawson

1944 *Johnny Tremain,* Esther Forbes, illus. Lynd Ward

1943 *Adam of the Road,* Elizabeth Janet Gray, illus. Robert Lawson

1942 *The Matchlock Gun,* Walter D. Edmonds, illus. Paul Lantz

1941 *Call It Courage,* Armstrong Sperry

1940 *Daniel Boone,* James Daugherty

1939 *Thimble Summer,* Elizabeth Enright

1938 *The White Stag,* Kate Seredy

1937 *Roller Skates,* Ruth Sawyer, illus. Valenti Angelo

1936 *Caddie Woodlawn,* Carol Ryrie Brink, illus. Kate Seredy

1935 *Dobry,* Monica Shannon, illus. Atanas Katchamakoff

1934 *Invincible Louisa: The Story of the Author of Little Women,* Cornelia L. Meigs

1933 *Young Fu of the Upper Yangtze,* Elizabeth Foreman Lewis, illus. Kurt Wiese

1932 *Waterless Mountain,* Laura Adams Armer, illus. Sydney Armer and Laura Adams Armer

1931 *The Cat Who Went to Heaven,* Elizabeth Coatsworth, illus. Lynd Ward

1930 *Hitty, Her First Hundred Years,* Rachel Field, illus. Dorothy P. Lathrop

1929 *The Trumpeter of Krakow,* Eric P. Kelly, illus. Angela Pruszynska

1928 *Gay-Neck: The Story of a Pigeon,* Dhan Gopal Mukerji, illus. Boris Artzybasheff

1927 *Smoky, the Cowhorse,* Will James

1926 *Shen of the Sea,* Arthur Bowie Chrisman, illus. Else Hasselriis

1925 *Tales from Silver Lands,* Charles Joseph Finger, illus. Paul Honore

1924 *The Dark Frigate,* Charles Boardman Hawes, illus. A.L. Ripley

1923 *The Voyages of Doctor Dolittle,* Hugh Lofting

1922 *The Story of Mankind,* Hendrik Willem Van Loon

Newbery Honor Books

٢♠

Runners-up for the distinction of being the best American children's book of the year are often as popular with children and adults as are the medal winners. Their book jackets proudly bear a foil sticker that sets them apart from other books. Because of the large number, just ten years' worth of books are included here.

1996   *The Great Fire,* Jim Murphy
        The Watsons Go to Birmingham—1963, Christopher Paul Curtis
        What Jamie Saw, Carolyn Coman
        Yolonda's Genius, Carol Fenner

1995   *Catherine, Called Birdy,* Karen Cushman
        The Ear, the Eye and the Arm, Nancy Farmer

1994   *Crazy Lady!,* Jane Leslie Conly
        Dragon's Gate, Laurence Yep
        Eleanor Roosevelt: A Life of Discovery, Russell Freedman

1993   *The Dark-Thirty: Southern Tales of the Supernatural,* Patricia C. McKissack
        Somewhere in the Darkness, Walter Dean Myers
        What Hearts, Bruce Brooks

1992   *Nothing but the Truth,* Avi
        The Wright Brothers: How They Invented the Airplane, Russell Freedman

1991   *The True Confessions of Charlotte Doyle,* Avi, illus. Ruth E. Murray

1990   *Afternoon of the Elves,* Janet Taylor Lisle
        Shabanu: Daughter of the Wind, Suzanne Fisher Staples
        The Winter Room, Gary Paulsen

1989 *In the Beginning: Creation Stories from Around the World,*
Virginia Hamilton, illus. Barry Moser
Scorpions, Walter Dean Myers

1988 *After the Rain,* Norma Fox Mazer
Hatchet, Gary Paulsen

1987 *A Fine White Dust,* Cynthia Rylant
On My Honor, Marion Dane Bauer
Volcano: The Eruption and Healing of Mount St. Helens,
Patricia Lauber

New York Academy of Sciences Children's Science Book Award

ॐ

Science writing for young people is promoted by this award. Winning books capture a unique perspective on animals, evolution, earth history, and outer space. Awards are given for books in two age categories: those appealing to primary-school students, ages 5 to 9, and those for older children, ages 9 through 16. First given in 1972, the award was suspended in 1990.

Ages 5 to 9

1989 *The Sierra Club Wayfinding Book,* Vicki McVey, illus. Martha Weston

1988 No award

1987 *Icebergs and Glaciers,* Seymour Simon

1986 *When Sheep Cannot Sleep,* Satoshi Kitamura

1985 *The Big Stretch: The Complete Book of the Amazing Rubber Band,* Ada Graham and Frank Graham, illus. Richard Rosenblum

1984 *The Secret Language of Snow,* Terry Tempest Williams and Ted Major, illus. Jennifer Dewey

1983 *Oak & Company,* Richard Mabey, illus. Clare Roberts

1982 *The Snail's Spell,* Joanne Ryder, illus. Lynne Cherry

1981 *Messing Around with Water Pumps and Siphons,* Bernie Zubrowski, illus. Steve Lindblom

1980 *Bet You Can't!: Science Impossibilities to Fool You,* Vicki Cobb and Kathy Darling, illus. Martha Weston

1979 *A Space Story,* Karla Kuskin, illus. Marc Simont

1978   *The Smallest Life Around Us,* Lucia Anderson, illus. Leigh Grant

1977   *Wild Mouse,* Irene Brady

1976   *Corn Is Maize: The Gift of the Indians,* Aliki

1975   *Emperor Penguin: Bird of the Antarctic,* Jean-Claude Deguine

1974   *See What I Am,* Roger Duvoisin

1973   *The Web in the Grass,* Berniece Freschet, illus. Roger Duvoisin

1972   *City Leaves, City Trees,* Edward Gallob

Ages 9 to 16

1989   *Digging Dinosaurs,* James Gorman and John R. Horner, illus. Kris Ellingsen and Donna Braginetz

1988   No award

1987   *Exploring the Night Sky: The Equinox Astronomy Guide for Beginners,* Terence Dickinson, illus. John Bianchi

1986   *The Evolution Book,* Sara Stein, illus. Rona Beame

1985   *Breakthrough: The True Story of Penicillin,* Francine Jacobs

1984   *The Daywatchers,* Peter Parnall

1983   *Volcano Weather: The Story of 1816, the Year Without a Summer,* Henry Stommel and Elizabeth Stommel

1982   *The Brooklyn Bridge: They Said It Couldn't Be Built,* Judith St. George

1981   *The Tree of Animal Life: A Tale of Changing Forms and Fortunes,* John C. McLoughlin

1980   *Moving Heavy Things,* Jan Adkins

1979   *Building: The Fight Against Gravity,* Mario Salvadori, illus. Saralinda Hooker and Christopher Ragus

1978   *Laser Light,* Herman Schneider, illus. Radu Vero

1977   *Grains: An Illustrated History with Recipes,* Elizabeth Burton Brown

1976   *Watching the Wild Apes: The Primate Studies of Goodall, Fossey, and Galdikas,* Bettyann Kevles

1975   *Doctor in the Zoo,* Bruce Buchenholz

1974   *Hunters of the Whale: An Adventure in Northwest Coast Archaelogy,* Richard D. Daugherty with Ruth Kirk, illus. Ruth Kirk and Louis Kirk

1973   *A Natural History of Giraffes,* Dorcas MacClintock, illus. Ugo Mochi

1972   *Reading the Past: The Story of Deciphering Ancient Languages,* Leonard Cottrell

1971   *The Stars and Serendipity,* Robert S. Richardson

The New York Times Best Illustrated Children's Books of the Year

ॐ

Remarkable picture books for all ages are honored in this well-publicized list. The books are chosen by the children's book editor of *The New York Times*, along with the help of a critic and an artist. Because of their number, only tens years' worth of books are listed below.

1995   *Alphabet City,* Stephen T. Johnson
      Buz, Richard Egielski
      Dogs Everywhere, Cor Hazelaar
      Kashtanka, Anton Chekov, trans. Ronald Meyer, illus. Gennady Spirin
      My Mama Had a Dancing Heart, Libba Moore Gray, illus. Raúl Colón
      She's Wearing a Dead Bird on Her Head!, Kathryn Lasky, illus. David Catrow
      Someplace Else, Carol P. Saul, illus. Barry Root
      When the Whippoorwill Calls, Candice F. Ransome, illus. Kimberly Bulcken Root
      Why the Sun and the Moon Live in the Sky, Niki Daly
      Zin! Zin! Zin! a Violin, Lloyd Moss, illus. Marjorie Priceman

1994   *The Boy and the Cloth of Dreams,* Jenny Koralek, illus. James Mayhew
      The Boy Who Ate Around, Henrik Drescher
      How Georgie Radbourn Saved Baseball, David Shannon
      My House, Lisa Desimini
      Ship of Dreams, Dean Morrissey
      The Sunday Outing, Gloria Jean Pinkney, illus. Jerry Pinkney
      Swamp Angel, Anne Isaacs, illus. Paul O. Zelinsky
      A Teeny Tiny Baby, Amy Schwartz

The Three Golden Keys, Peter Sis
The Wave of the Sea-Wolf, David Wisniewski

1993 *The Bracelet,* Yoshiko Uchida, illus. Joanna Yardley
Grandfather's Journey, Allen Say
Gulliver's Adventures in Lilliput, Jonathan Swift, retold by
Ann Keay Beneduce, illus. Gennady Spirin
Harvey Slumfenburger's Christmas Present, John Burningham
How Dogs Really Work!, Alan Snow
Hue Boy, Rita Phillips Mitchell, illus. Caroline Binch
A Number of Animals, Christopher Wormell
The Perilous Pit, Orel Odinov Protopopescu, illus. Jacqueline
Chwast
A Small Tall Tale from the Far Far North, Peter Sis
Stephen Biesty's Cross-Sections: Man-of-War, Richard Platt,
illus. Stephen Biesty

1992 *Boodil, My Dog,* Pija Lindenbaum, retold by Gabrielle
Charbonnet
The Cataract of Lodore, Robert Southey, illus. David Catrow
The Fortune-Tellers, Lloyd Alexander, illus. Trina Schart Hyman
*Li'l Sis and Uncle Willie: A Story Based on the Life and
Paintings of William H. Johnson,* Gwen Everett, illus. William
H. Johnson
Martha Speaks, Susan Meddaugh
Mirette on the High Wire, Emily Arnold McCully
Oscar de Mejo's ABC, Oscar de Mejo
The Stinky Cheese Man and Other Fairly Stupid Tales, Jon
Scieszka, illus. Lane Smith
Where Does It Go?, Margaret Miller
Why the Sky Is Far Away: A Folktale from Nigeria, Mary-Joan
Gerson, illus. Carla Golembe

1991 *Another Celebrated Dancing Bear,* Gladys Scheffrin-Falk, illus.
Barbara Garrison
Diego, Jonah Winter, trans. Amy Prince, illus. Jeanette Winter
Follow the Dream: The Story of Christoper Columbus, Peter Sis

Little Red Riding Hood, Charles Perrault, retold and illus.
Beni Montresor
Old Mother Hubbard and Her Wonderful Dog, Sarah
Catherine Martin, illus. James Marshall
Ooh-La-La (Max in Love), Maira Kalman
Punch in New York, Alice Provensen
Tar Beach, Faith Ringgold
The Marvelous Journey Through the Night, Helme Heine
What Can Rabbit Hear?, Lucy Cousins

1990 *Beach Ball,* Peter Sis
Beneath a Blue Umbrella, Jack Prelutsky, illus. Garth Williams
A Christmas Carol, Charles Dickens, illus. Roberto Innocenti
The Dancing Palm Tree and Other Nigerian Folktales, Barbara
K. Walker, illus. Helen Siegl
Fish Eyes: A Book You Can Count On, Lois Ehlert
I'm Flying!, Alan Wade, illus. Petra Mathers
The Fool and the Fish: A Tale from Russia, Alexander
Nikolayevich Afanasyev, illus. Gennady Spirin
One Gorilla: A Counting Book, Atsuko Morozumi
The Tale of the Mandarin Ducks, Katherine Paterson, illus.
Leo Dillon and Diane Dillon
War Boy: A Country Childhood, Michael Foreman

1989 *The Dancing Skeleton,* Cynthia C. DeFelice, illus. Robert
Andrew Parker
Does God Have a Big Toe? Stories about Stories in the Bible,
Marc Gellman, illus. Oscar de Mejo
The Heartaches of a French Cat, Barbara McClintock
How Pizza Came to Queens, Dayal Kaur Khalsa
Nicholas Cricket, Joyce Maxner, illus. William Joyce
Olson's Meat Pies, Peter Cohen, illus. Olof Landstrom
Peacock Pie: A Book of Rhymes, Walter de la Mare, illus.
Louise Brierley
Theseus and the Minotaur, Warwick Hutton
Turtle in July, Marilyn Singer, illus. Jerry Pinkney
Whales, Seymour Simon

1988   *Cats Are Cats: Poems,* Nancy Larrick, illus. Ed Young
       Fire Came to the Earth People, Susan L. Roth
       I Want to Be an Astronaut, Byron Barton
       Look! Look! Look!, Tana Hoban
       A River Dream, Allen Say
       Shaka: King of the Zulus, Peter Vennema and Diane Stanley,
       illus. Diane Stanley
       Sir Francis Drake: His Daring Deeds, Roy Gerrard
       Stringbean's Trip to the Shining Sea, Vera B. Williams, illus.
       Vera B. Williams and Jennifer Williams
       Swan Sky, Keizaburo Tejima
       Theodor and Mr. Balbini, Petra Mathers

1987   *The Cremation of Sam McGee,* Robert W. Service, illus. Ted
       Harrison
       Fox's Dream, Keizaburo Tejima
       Halloween ABC, Eve Merriam, illus. Lane Smith
       *Handtalk Birthday: A Number and Story Book in Sign
       Language,* Remy Charlip and Mary Beth Miller, illus. George
       Ancona
       In Coal Country, Judith Hendershot, illus. Thomas B. Allen
       Jump Again! More Adventures of Brer Rabbit, Joel Chandler
       Harris, adapted by Van Dyne Parks, illus. Barry Moser
       The Mountains of Tibet, Mordicai Gerstein
       Rainbow Rhino, Peter Sis
       Seventeen Kings and Forty-Two Elephants, Margaret Mahy,
       illus. Patricia McCarthy
       The Yellow Umbrella, Henrik Drescher

1986   *Brave Irene,* William Steig
       Cherries and Cherry Pits, Vera B. Williams
       Flying, Donald Crews
       Molly's New Washing Machine, Laura Geringer, illus. Petra
       Mathers
       One Morning, Canna Funakoshi, illus. Yohiji Izawa
       The Owl-Scatterer, Howard Norman, illus. Michael McCurdy
       Pigs from A to Z, Arthur Geisert

Rembrandt Takes a Walk, Mark Strand, illus. Red Grooms
The Stranger, Chris Van Allsburg
The Ugly Duckling, Hans Christian Andersen, illus. Robert Van Nutt

Scott O'Dell Award for Historical Fiction

෨

Historical fiction set in the New World (North, South, or Central America) is celebrated by this award. The $5,000 prize, first given in 1984, is administered by the Scott O'Dell Foundation. O'Dell was the recipient of numerous prizes for such books as *Island of the Blue Dolphins* and *The Black Pearl*. He also won the prestigious Hans Christian Andersen Award.

1996   *The Bomb,* Theodore Taylor

1995   *Under the Blood-Red Sun,* Graham Salisbury

1994   *Bull Run,* Paul Fleischman

1993   *Morning Girl,* Michael Dorris

1992   *Stepping on the Cracks,* Mary Downing Hahn

1991   *A Time of Troubles,* Pieter van Raven

1990   *Shades of Gray,* Carolyn Reeder

1989   *The Honorable Prison,* Lyll Becerra de Jenkins

1988   *Charley Skedaddle,* Patricia Beatty

1987   *Streams to the River, River to the Sea,* Scott O'Dell

1986   *Sarah, Plain and Tall,* Patricia MacLachlan

1985   *The Fighting Ground,* Avi

1984   *The Sign of the Beaver,* Elizabeth George Speare

Orbis Pictus Award for Outstanding Nonfiction for Children

ɜ&

Distinguished nonfiction is featured in the list of these winners. The award itself commemorates what is thought to be the first children's book, *Orbis Pictus* (*The World in Pictures*), authored by Johannes Amos Comenius and published in 1657. The award is administered by the National Council of Teachers of English and is given for a book considered useful in classroom teaching.

1996   *The Great Fire,* Jim Murphy

1995   *Safari Beneath the Sea: The Wonder of the North Pacific Coast,*
Diane Swanson

1994   *Across America on an Emigrant Train,* Jim Murphy

1993   *Children of the Dust Bowl: The True Story of the School at
Weedpatch Camp,* Jerry Stanley

1992   *Flight: The Journey of Charles Lindbergh,* Robert Burleigh,
illus. Mike Wimmer

1991   *Franklin Delano Roosevelt,* Russell Freedman

1990   *The Great Little Madison,* Jean Fritz

Phoenix Award

ஃ

A 20-year-old book which suffers from neglect is highlighted by this unique award. Named for the fabled bird that rises from the ashes to renewed life, the prize honors a book that did not win a major award at publication date. Yet its timeless literary merit is deemed worthy of special recognition two decades later by the teachers, scholars, librarians, and parents who belong to the Children's Literature Association.

1996 *The Stone Book,* Alan Garner

1995 *Dragonwings,* Laurence Yep

1994 *Of Nightingales That Weep,* Katherine Paterson

1993 *Carrie's War,* Nina Bawden, illus. Coleen Browning

1992 *A Sound of Chariots,* Mollie Hunter

1991 *A Long Way from Verona,* Jane Gardam

1990 *Enchantress from the Stars,* Sylvia Louise Engdahl, illus. Rodney Shackell

1989 *The Night Watchmen,* Helen Cresswell, illus. Gareth Floyd

1988 *The Rider and His Horse,* Erik Christian Haugaard, illus. Leo Dillon and Diane Dillon

1987 *Smith,* Leon Garfield, illus. Antony Maitland

1986 *Queenie Peavy,* Robert Burch, illus. Jerry Lazare

1985 *The Mark of the Horse Lord,* Rosemary Sutcliff

Please Touch Museum Book Award

❧

Very young children, ages 3 and younger, delight in these winning books. Featured are bright pictures and simple tasks that aim to teach something, such as counting. The award was begun in 1985 by the Philadelphia museum of the same name. In 1995 a counterpart for children ages 4 to 7 was launched.

Ages 3 and Under

1995 *Hippity Hop, Frog on Top,* Natasha Wing, illus. DeLoss McGraw

1994 *Arnold Always Answers,* Deborah Kotter

1993 *Fiddle-I-Fee,* Melissa Sweet

1992 *In the Tall, Tall Grass,* Denise Fleming

1991 *Maisy Goes to Bed,* Lucy Cousins

1990 *Dinosaurs, Dinosaurs,* Byron Barton

1989 *Who's Sick Today?,* Lynne Cherry

1988 *Claude and Sun,* Matt Novak

1987 *Who's Counting,* Nancy Tafuri

1986 *Is It Larger? Is It Smaller?,* Tana Hoban

1985 *What's Inside?,* Duanne Daughty

Ages 4 to 7

1995 *Prize in the Snow,* Bill Easterling, illus. Mary Beth Owens

Romance Writers of America RITA Award

Romance writing embraces almost half of all mass-market fiction sales. This writing is gloried by an award named for the cofounder and first president of the Romance Writers of America, Rita Clay Estrada. The RITA is awarded for several categories of romance writing, including young adult romance. In July, winners receive a gold RITA statuette.

1995   *Second to None*, Arlynn Presser

1994   *Summer Lightning*, Wendy Corsi Staub

1993   *Song of the Buffalo Boy*, Sherry Garland

1992   *Now I Lay Me Down to Sleep*, Lurlene McDaniel

1991   No award

1990   *Renee*, Vivian Schurfranz

1989   *The Ghosts of Stony Cove*, Eileen Charbonneau

1988   *Does Your Nose Get in the Way, Too?*, Arlene Erlbach

1987   *Video Fever*, Kathleen Garvey

1986   *Waiting for Amanda*, Cheryl Zach

1985   *The Frog Princess*, Cheryl Zach

1984   *Julie's Magic Moment*, Barbara Bartholomew

1983   *Andrea*, Jo Steward

Smarties Book Prize

Light-hearted stories are honored by this prize named after Britain's top-selling confection. Administered by the Book Trust, the prize is granted by a panel of grown-ups who have been coached by students. Funded by Nestlé, the prize carries the biggest purse of any children's award. There are several winning categories, but the overall winner receives the equivalent of $12,000.

1995 *Double Act,* Jacqueline Wilson

1994 *The Exiles at Home,* Hilary McKay

1993 *War Game,* Michael Foreman

1992 *The Great Elephant Chase,* Gillian Cross

1991 *Farmer Duck,* Martin Waddell, illus. Helen Oxenbury

1990 *Midnight Blue,* Pauline Fisk

1989 *We're Going on a Bear Hunt,* Michael Rosen, illus. Helen Oxenbury

1988 *Can't You Sleep, Little Bear?,* Martin Waddell, illus. Barbara Firth

1987 *A Thief in the Village,* James Berry

1986 *The Snow Spider,* Jenny Nimmo, illus. Joanne Carey

1985 *Gaffer Samson's Luck,* Jill Paton Walsh, illus. Brock Cole

Mark Twain Award

Pranks and perils in the lives of young people are often central to the books winning this award. Missouri schoolchildren, ages 9 to 13, choose their favorite from a list of 20 titles drawn up by various reading and children organizations in the state. Started in 1972, the award is named for Missouri's best-known literary figure (born Samuel Clemens), creator of Tom Sawyer and Huckleberry Finn.

1996   *The Ghosts of Mercy Manor,*   Betty Ren Wright

1995   *The Man Who Loved Clowns,*   June Rae Wood

1994   *Shiloh,*   Phyllis Reynolds Naylor

1993   *Maniac Magee,*   Jerry Spinelli

1992   *The Doll in the Garden: A Ghost Story,*   Mary Downing Hahn

1991   *All About Sam,*   Lois Lowry

1990   *There's a Boy in the Girls' Bathroom,*   Louis Sachar

1989   *Sixth-Grade Sleepover,*   Eve Bunting

1988   *Baby-Sitting Is a Dangerous Job,*   Willo Davis Roberts

1987   *The War with Grandpa,*   Robert Kimmel Smith, illus. Richard Lauter

1986   *The Dollhouse Murders,*   Betty Ren Wright

1985   *A Bundle of Sticks,*   Pat Rhoads Mauser, illus. Gail Owens

1984   *The Secret Life of the Underwear Champ,*   Betty Miles, illus. Dan Jones

1983   *The Girl with the Silver Eyes,*   Willo Davis Roberts

1982   *The Boy Who Saw Bigfoot,* Marian T. Place

1981   *Soup for President,* Robert Newton Peck, illus. Ted Lewin

1980   *The Pinballs,* Betsy Byars

1979   *The Champion of Merrimack County,* Roger W. Drury, illus. Fritz Wegner

1978   *Ramona the Brave,* Beverly Cleary, illus. Alan Tiegreen

1977   *The Ghost on Saturday Night,* Sid Fleischman, illus. Eric von Schmidt

1976   *The Home Run Trick,* Scott Corbett, illus. Paul Galdone

1975   *How to Eat Fried Worms,* Thomas Rockwell, illus. Emily Arnold McCully

1974   *It's a Mile from Here to Glory,* Robert C. Lee

1973   *Mrs. Frisby and the Rats of NIMH,* Robert C. O'Brien, illus. Zena Bernstein

1972   *Sounder,* William H. Armstrong, illus. James Barkley

Western Heritage Award

೭♣

To encourage writers who spin tales of the American West, the National Cowboy Hall of Fame and the Western Heritage Center created this award. The books are funny, wild, and offer a unique perspective for a juvenile audience. Winners lasso a Wrangler trophy, a bronze sculpture of a cowboy on his horse.

1996   *The Night the Grandfathers Danced*, Linda Raczek

1995   *Eagle Drum*, Robert Crum

1994   *Cowboys, Indians and Gunfighters*, Albert Marrin

1993   *An Indian Winter*, Russell Freedman

1992   *Monster Slayer: A Navajo Folktale*, retold by Vee Brown, illus. Baje Whitethorne

1991   *Bunkhouse Journal*, Diane Johnston Hamm

1990   *Letters to Oma: A Young German Girl's Account of Her First Year in Texas, 1847*, Marj Gurasich, illus. Barbara Whitehead

1989   *Stay Put, Robbie McAmis*, Frances G. Tunbo, illus. Charles Shaw

1988   *The Covered Wagon and Other Adventures*, Lynn H. Scott

1987   *Happily May I Walk: American Indians and Alaska Natives Today*, Arlene Hirschfelder

1986   *Prairie Songs*, Pam Conrad, illus. Darryl S. Zudeck

1985   No award

1984   *Children of the Wild West*, Russell Freedman

1981–1983   No awards

1980   *The Little House Cookbook,* Barbara M. Walker, illus. Garth Williams

1979   *The Obstinate Land,* Harold Keith

1977–1978   No award

1976   *Owl in the Cedar Tree,* Natachee Scott Momaday, illus. Don Perceval

1975   *Susy's Scoundrel,* Harold Keith, illus. John Schoenherr

1974   No award

1973   *Famous American Explorers,* Bern Keating, illus. Lorence F. Bjorklund

1972   *The Black Mustanger,* Richard Wormser, illus. Donald Bolognese

1971   *And One Was a Wooden Indian,* Betty Baker

1970   *An Awful Name to Live Up To,* Jossie Hosford, illus. Charles Geer

1969   *Edge of Two Worlds,* Weyman Jones, illus. J.C. Kocsis

1968   *Down the River, Westward Ho!,* Eric Scott

1967   *Mustang: Wild Spirit of the West,* Marguerite Henry, illus. Robert Lougheed

1966   *Land Rush,* Carl G. Hodges, illus. John Martinez

1965   *The Greatest Cattle Drive,* Paul I. Wellman, illus. Lorence F. Bjorklund

1964   *Killer-of-Death,* Betty Baker, illus. John Kaufmann

1963   *The Book of the West: An Epic of America's Wild Frontier,* Charles Chilton, illus. Eric Tansley

1962   *King of the Mountain Men: The Life of Jim Bridger,* Gene Caesar

Whitbread Award

&

Popularity with children in Great Britain and Ireland is key to the novels winning this award. Named for and funded by the big brewer, Whitbread Plc, this rich award is administered by the Booksellers Association of Great Britain and Ireland. Winners receive more than $3,000.

1995   *The Wreck of the Zanzibar*, Michael Morpurgo

1994   *Gold Dust*, Geraldine McCaughrean

1993   *Flour Babies*, Anne Fine

1992   *The Great Elephant Chase*, Gillian Cross

1991   *Harvey Angell*, Diana Hendry

1990   *AK*, Peter Dickinson

1989   *Why Weeps the Brogan?*, Hugh Scott

1988   *Awaiting Developments*, Judy Allen

1987   *A Little Lower than the Angels*, Geraldine McCaughrean

1986   *The Coal House*, Andrew Taylor

1985   *The Nature of the Beast*, Janni Howker

1984   *The Queen of Pharisees' Children*, Barbara Willard

1983   *The Witches*, Roald Dahl, illus. Quentin Blake

1982   *The Song of Pentecost*, William J. Corbett, illus. Martin Unsell

1981   *The Hollow Land*, Jane Gardam, illus. Janet Rawlins

1980   *John Diamond*, Leon Garfield, illus. Antony Maitland

1979   *Tulku,*   Peter Dickinson

1978   *The Battle of Bubble and Squeak,*   A. Philippa Pearce, illus. Alan Baker

1977   *No End to Yesterday,*   Shelagh Macdonald

1976   *A Stitch in Time,*   Penelope Lively

1975   No award

1974   *The Emperor's Winding Sheet,*   Jill Paton Walsh
        How Tom Beat Captain Najork and His Hired Sportsmen, Russell Hoban, illus. Quentin Blake

1973   *The Butterfly Ball and the Grasshopper's Feast,*   William Plomer, illus. Alan Aldridge

1972   *The Diddakoi,*   Rumer Godden, illus. Creina Glegg

William Allen White Children's Book Award

୨**ଏ**

A flavor of the Midwest pervades the winners of this award. That's probably because the winners are chosen by more than 50,000 Kansas schoolchildren. Named after the distinguished Kansas journalist, winner of two Pulitzer Prizes for his writing during the first half of the twentieth century, the award features books suitable for 9- to 13-year-olds.

1995   *The Man Who Loved Clowns,* June Rae Wood

1994   *Shiloh,* Phyllis Reynolds Naylor

1993   *Maniac Magee,* Jerry Spinelli

1992   *The Doll in the Garden: A Ghost Story,* Mary Downing Hahn

1991   *Beauty,* Bill Wallace

1990   *Hatchet,* Gary Paulsen

1989   *On My Honor,* Marion Dane Bauer

1988   *Cracker Jackson,* Betsy Byars

1987   *The War with Grandpa,* Robert Kimmel Smith, illus. Richard Lauter

1986   *Daphne's Book,* Mary Downing Hahn

1985   *The Land I Lost: Adventures of a Boy in Vietnam,* Huynh Quang Nhuong, illus. Vo-Dinh Mai

1984   *A Light in the Attic,* Shel Silverstein

1983   *Peppermints in the Parlor,* Barbara Brooks Wallace

1982   *The Magic of the Glits,* Carole S. Adler, illus. Ati Forberg

1981   *The Great Gilly Hopkins,* Katherine Paterson

1980   *The Pinballs,* Betsy Byars

1979   *Summer of the Monkeys,* Wilson Rawls

1978   *The Great Christmas Kidnapping Caper,* Jean Van Leeuwen, illus. Steven Kellogg

1977   *Harry Cat's Pet Puppy,* George Selden, illus. Garth Williams

1976   *Socks,* Beverly Cleary, illus. Beatrice Darwin

1975   *Dominic,* William Steig

1974   *The Headless Cupid,* Zilpha Keatley Snyder, illus. Alton Raible
       Mrs. Frisby and the Rats of NIMH, Robert C. O'Brien, illus. Zena Bernstein

1973   *The Trumpet of the Swan,* E.B. White, illus. Edward Frascino

1972   *Sasha, My Friend,* Barbara Corcoran, illus. Richard L. Shell

1971   *Kavik the Wolf Dog,* Walt Morey, illus. Peter Parnall

1970   *From the Mixed-up Files of Mrs. Basil E. Frankweiler,* E.L. Konigsburg

1969   *Henry Reed's Babysitting Service,* Keith Robertson, illus. Robert McCloskey

1968   *The Mouse and the Motorcycle,* Beverly Cleary, illus. Louis Darling

1967   *The Grizzly,* Annabel Johnson and Edgar Johnson, illus. Gilbert Riswold

1966   *Rascal: A Memoir of a Better Era,* Sterling North, illus. John Schoenherr

1965   *Bristle Face,* Zachary Ball

1964   *The Incredible Journey: A Tale of Three Animals,* Sheila Every Burnford, illus. Carl Burger

1963 *Island of the Blue Dolphins,* Scott O'Dell

1962 *The Helen Keller Story,* Catherine O. Peare

1961 *Henry Reed, Inc.,* Keith Robertson, illus. Robert McCloskey

1960 *Flaming Arrows,* William O. Steele, illus. Paul Galdone

1959 *Old Yeller,* Fred Gipson, illus. Carl Burger

1958 *White Falcon,* Elliott Arnold, illus. Frederick T. Chapman

1957 *Daniel 'Coon: The Story of a Pet Racoon,* Phoebe Erickson

1956 *Brighty of the Grand Canyon,* Marguerite Henry, illus. Wesley Dennis

1955 *Cherokee Bill: Oklahoma Pacer,* Jean Bailey, illus. Pers Crowell

1954 *Little Vic,* Doris Gates, illus. Kate Seredy

1953 *Amos Fortune, Free Man,* Elizabeth Yates, illus. Nora S. Unwin

Laura Ingalls Wilder Award

Authors or illustrators whose entire body of work has made a lasting and substantial contribution to American children's literature are given this honor. It is named for America's well-loved chronicler of life on the American frontier, which was captured in her autobiographical *Little House* series. The award is now given every three years by the Association of Library Services to Children.

1995   Virginia Hamilton

1992   Marcia Brown

1989   Elizabeth George Speare

1986   Jean Fritz

1983   Maurice Sendak

1980   Dr. Seuss (Theodor S. Geisel)

1975   Beverly Cleary

1970   E.B. White

1965   Ruth Sawyer

1960   Clara Ingram Judson

1954   Laura Ingalls Wilder

Young Reader's Choice Award

ता

Children in the Pacific Northwest vote for winners of this, the oldest children's choice book award. The prize list includes such well-loved classic titles as *Lassie Come Home* and *The Black Stallion,* which show up on surprisingly few other award lists. Another roster to honor books aimed at older teenagers was added in 1991.

Ages 9 to 14

1996   *The Boys Start the War* and *The Girls Get Even,* Phyllis Reynolds Naylor

1995   *Terror at the Zoo,* Peg Kehret

1994   *Shiloh,* Phyllis Reynolds Naylor

1993   *Maniac Magee,* Jerry Spinelli

1992   *Danger in Quicksand Swamp,* Bill Wallace

1991   *Ten Kids, No Pets,* Ann M. Martin

1990   *There's a Boy in the Girls' Bathroom,* Louis Sachar

1989   *Wait Till Helen Comes: A Ghost Story,* Mary Downing Hahn

1988   *Sixth Grade Can Really Kill You,* Barthe DeClements

1987   *The War with Grandpa,* Robert Kimmel Smith, illus. Richard Lauter

1986   *The Dollhouse Murders,* Betty Ren Wright

1985   *Thirteen Ways to Sink a Sub,* Jamie Gilson, illus. Linda S. Edwards

1984   *The Indian in the Cupboard,* Lynn Reid Banks, illus. Brock Cole

1983   *Superfudge,* Judy Blume

1982   *Bunnicula: A Rabbit-Tale of Mystery,* Deborah Howe and James Howe, illus. Alan Daniel

1981   *Hail, Hail, Camp Timberwood,* Ellen Conford, illus. Gail Owens

1980   *Ramona and Her Father,* Beverly Cleary, illus. Alan Tiegreen

1979   *Roll of Thunder, Hear My Cry,* Mildred D. Taylor, illus. Jerry Pinkney

1978   *The Great Brain Does It Again,* John D. Fitzgerald, illus. Mercer Mayer

1977   *Blubber,* Judy Blume

1976   *The Great Brain Reforms,* John D. Fitzgerald, illus. Mercer Mayer

1975   *Tales of a Fourth Grade Nothing,* Judy Blume, illus. Roy Doty

1974   *Mrs. Frisby and the Rats of NIMH,* Robert C. O'Brien, illus. Zena Bernstein

1973   No award

1972   *Encyclopedia Brown Keeps the Peace,* Donald J. Sobol, illus. Leonard Shortall

1971   *Ramona the Pest,* Beverly Cleary, illus. Louis Darling

1970   *Smoke,* William Corbin

1969   *Henry Reed's Babysitting Service,* Keith Robertson, illus. Robert McCloskey

1968   *The Mouse and the Motorcycle,* Beverly Cleary, illus. Louis Darling

1967   *Chitty-Chitty-Bang-Bang,* Ian Fleming, illus. John Burningham

1966   *Rascal: A Memoir of a Better Era,* Sterling North, illus. John Schoenherr

1965   *John F. Kennedy and PT-109*, Richard Tregaskis

1964   *The Incredible Journey: A Tale of Three Animals*, Sheila Every Burnford, illus. Carl Burger

1963   *Danny Dunn on the Ocean Floor*, Jay Williams and Raymond Abrashkin, illus. Brinton Turkle

1962   *The Swamp Fox of the Revolution*, Stewart Holbrook, illus. Ernest Richardson

1961   *Danny Dunn and the Homework Machine*, Jay Williams and Raymond Abrashkin, illus. Ezra Jack Keats

1960   *Henry and the Paper Route*, Beverly Cleary, illus. Louis Darling

1959   *Old Yeller*, Fred Gipson, illus. Carl Burger

1958   *Golden Mare*, William Corbin, illus. Pers Crowell

1957   *Henry and Ribsy*, Beverly Cleary, illus. Louis Darling

1956   *Miss Pickerell Goes to Mars*, Ellen MacGregor, illus. Paul Galdone

1953–1955 No awards

1952   *Sea Star: Orphan of Chincoteague*, Marguerite Henry, illus. Wesley Dennis

1951   *King of the Wind*, Marguerite Henry, illus. Wesley Dennis

1950   *McElligot's Pool*, Dr. Seuss (Theodor S. Geisel)

1949   *Cowboy Boots*, Doris Shannon Garst, illus. Charles Hargens

1948   *The Black Stallion Returns*, Walter Farley, illus. Harold Eldridge

1947   *Homer Price*, Robert McCloskey

1946   *The Return of Silver Chief*, Jack O'Brien, illus. Kurt Wiese

1945   *Snow Treasure*, Marie McSwigan, illus. Mary Reardon

1944   *The Black Stallion*, Walter Farley, illus. Keith Ward

1943   *Lassie Come Home*, Eric Knight, illus. Cyrus L. Baldridge

1942   *By the Shores of Silver Lake*, Laura Ingalls Wilder, illus.
        Mildred Boyle and Helen Sewell

1941   *Mr. Popper's Penguins*, Florence Atwater and Richard Atwate
        illus. Robert Lawson

1940   *Paul Bunyan Swings His Axe*, Dell J. McCormick

Ages 15 to 18

1996   *The Giver*, Lois Lowry

1995   *Who Killed My Daughter*, Lois Duncan

1994   *Wolf by the Ears*, Ann Rinaldi

1993   *The Face on the Milk Carton*, Caroline B. Cooney

1992   *Eva*, Peter Dickinson

1991   *Sex Education*, Jenny Davis

Above the Rest

ॐ

Special recognition is given to books which have won multiple commendations in the nearly two hundred competitions reviewed by the editors in preparing *Literary Laurels: Kids' Edition.*

All About Sam, Lois Lowry

Are You There, God? It's Me, Margaret, Judy Blume

Baby-Sitting Is a Dangerous Job, Willo Davis Roberts

Bad Boy, Diana Wieler

Be a Perfect Person in Just Three Days!, Stephen Manes

The Best Christmas Pageant Ever, Barbara Robinson

Bill Peet: An Autobiography, Bill Peet

Bridge to Terabithia, Katherine Paterson

Bunnicula: A Rabbit-Tale of Mystery, Deborah Howe and James Howe

Christina's Ghost, Betty Ren Wright

Dear Mr. Henshaw, Beverly Cleary

The Dollhouse Murders, Betty Ren Wright

From the Mixed-Up Files of Mrs. Basil E. Frankweiler, E.L. Konigsburg

Fudge, Charlotte T. Graeber

The Garden of Abdul Gasazi, Chris Van Allsburg

Good Night, Mr. Tom, Michelle Magorian

Grandfather's Journey, Allen Say

The Great Gilly Hopkins, Katherine Paterson

Hatchet, Gary Paulsen

Have You Seen Birds?, Joanne Oppenheim

The Headless Cupid, Zilpha Keatley Snyder

Hold Fast, Kevin Major

How to Eat Friend Worms, Thomas Rockwell

If You Give a Mouse a Cookie, Laura Numeroff

In a Dark, Dark Room, and Other Scary Stories, Alvin Schwartz

The Incredible Journey: A Tale of Three Animals, Sheila Every Burnford

The Indian in the Cupboard, Lynne Reid Banks

Island of the Blue Dolphins, Scott O'Dell

The Magic Schoolbus at the Waterworks, Joanna Cole

Maniac Magee, Jerry Spinelli

Matilda, Roald Dahl

M.C. Higgins, the Great, Virginia Hamilton

Mrs. Frisby and the Rats of NIMH, Robert C. O'Brien

Mufaro's Beautiful Daughters: An African Tale, John Steptoe

Noah's Ark, Peter Spier

Nothing's Fair in Fifth Grade, Barthe DeClements

Number the Stars, Lois Lowry

Old Yeller, Fred Gipson

One-Eyed Cat, Paula Fox

The Other Side of Dark, Joan Lowery Nixon

The People Could Fly: American Black Folktales, Virginia Hamilton

The Pinballs, Betsy Byars

The Polar Express, Chris Van Allsburg

Queenie Peavey, Robert Burch

Ralph S. Mouse, Beverly Cleary

Ramona and Her Father, Beverly Cleary

Ramona Quimby, Age 8, Beverly Cleary

Rascal: A Memoir of a Better Era, John Schoenherr

The Road from Home: The Story of an Armenian Girl, David Kherdian

Sarah, Plain and Tall, Patricia MacLachlan

Shadow in Hawthorn Bay, Janet Lunn

Shiloh, Phyllis Reynolds Naylor

The Sign of the Beaver, Elizabeth George Speare

Sixth Grade Can Really Kill You, Barthe DeClements

Skinnybones, Barbara Park

So Much to Tell You, John Marsden

Sounder, William H. Armstrong

Stone Fox, John Reynolds Gardiner

Stranger with My Face, Lois Duncan

Summer of the Monkeys, Wilson Rawls

Superfudge, Judy Blume

Sweet Whispers, Brother Rush, Virginia Hamilton

Tales of a Fourth Grade Nothing, Judy Blume

Tar Beach, Faith Ringgold

There's a Boy in the Girls' Bathroom, Louis Sachar

Tiger Eyes, Judy Blume

The True Confessions of Charlotte Doyle, Avi

The Trumpet of the Swan, E.B. White

Wait Till Helen Comes: A Ghost Story, Mary Downing Hahn

The War with Grandpa, Robert Kimmel Smith

The Way Things Work, David Macaulay

Where the Forest Meets the Sea, Jeannie Baker

The Wright Brothers: How They Invented the Airplane, Russell Freedman

Children's Bookstores

࿇

Need help locating a hard-to-find or out-of-print title? Try these sources:

East Coast
Books of Wonder
132 Seventh Avenue
New York, NY 10011
Phone: (212) 989-3270
Fax: (212) 989-1203

Midwest
The Red Balloon Bookshop
891 Grand Avenue
Saint Paul, MN 55105
Phone: (612) 224-8320
Fax: (612) 224-9508

South
Haslam's Bookstore, Inc.
2025 Central Avenue
St. Petersburg, FL 33713
Phone: (813) 822-8616
Fax: (813) 822-7416

West Coast
Carol Docheff Bookseller (catalog available)
1390 Reliez Valley Road
Lafayette, CA 94549
Phone: (510) 935-9595

Canada
The Children's Bookstore
2532 Yonge Street
Toronto, Ontario M4P 2H7
Canada
Phone: (416) 480-0233
Fax: (416) 480-9345

United Kingdom
Harrods Ltd.
Children's Book Department
Knightsbridge, London SW1X 7XL
England
Phone: 011-44-171-225-5721
Fax: 011-44-171-225-5611

Hatchards
Children's Book Department
187 Piccadilly
London W1V 0LE
England
Phone: 011-44-171-439-9921 ext. 2300
Fax: 011-44-171-494-1313

Author/Illustrator Index

இஆ

Aardema, Verna, 16, 26
Abrashkin, Raymond, 98
Ackerman, Karen, 15
Ada, Alma Flor, 36
Adams, Adrienne, 32
Adams, Richard, 22
Adéle, Geras, 62
Adkins, Jan, 27, 73
Adler, Carole S., 49, 92
Adoff, Arnold, 61
Ahlberg, Allan, 54, 55
Ahlberg, Janet, 54, 55
Aiken, Joan, 30, 43
Akaba, Suekichi, 6
Alcott, Louisa May, 28
Aldridge, Alan, 91
Alexander, Lloyd, 13, 64, 67, 76
Alexander, Martha, 39
Alexander, Sally Hobart, 35
Aliki, 73
Allen, Agnes, 23
Allen, Jack, 23
Allen, Judy, 90
Allen, Thomas B., 78
Almagor, Gila, 62
Ambrus, Victor G., 12, 22, 55
Ancona, George, 78
Andersen, Hans Christian, 30, 32, 52, 79
Anderson, David A., 60
Anderson, Lucia, 73
Angelo, Valenti, 30, 69
Anno, Mitsumasa, 6, 13, 39
Ardizzone, Edward, 23, 26, 33, 56
Armer, Laura Adams, 69
Armer, Sydney, 69
Armstrong, Richard, 23
Armstrong, William H., 28, 67, 87, 102

Arnosky, Jim, 38
Arthur, Malcolm, 19
Artzybasheff, Boris, 69
Ashabranner, Brent K., 37
Ashabranner, Melissa, 37
Atkinson, Linda, 62
Atwater, Florence, 33, 99
Atwater, Richard, 33, 99
Aurora, Shirley L., 3
Avi, 10, 38, 48, 70, 80, 102
Ayer, Eleanor, 35
Azon, Gary, 59

Babbit, Natalie, 26, 39
Bailey, Carolyn Sherwin, 68
Bailey, Jean, 94
Baker, Alan, 91
Baker, Betty, 89
Baker, Charlotte, 26
Baker, Jeannie, 102
Baker, Keith, 50
Baldridge, Cyrus L., 99
Ball, Zachary, 46, 93
Bancroft, Griffing, 40
Bang, Molly, 13
Banks, Lynn Reid, 96, 101
Bannon, Laura, 34
Barkley, James, 28, 67, 87
Barne, Kitty, 24
Barrett, Jennifer, 37
Bartholomew, Barbara, 84
Barton, Byron, 78, 83
Bartone, Elisa, 19
Bauer, Caroline Feller, 38
Bauer, Marion Dane, 3, 71, 92
Baum, L. Frank, 29
Baumann, Hans, 9

Title Index

&

121

Title Index

Title Index